THE POLICE AND CRIMINAL EVIDENCE ACT 1984: THE ROLE OF THE APPROPRIATE ADULT

Brian Littlechild

BASW

**BRITISH ASSOCIATION
OF SOCIAL WORKERS**

BASW PUBLICATIONS

The Police and Criminal Evidence Act 1984: The Role of the Appropriate Adul

Includes new codes of Practice, 1991 and 1995, Codes on Tape Recording of Interviews, and Criminal Justice Act 1991 legislation on transfer of juveniles to local authority care, with notes on the roles of interpreters.   *Brian Littlechild*

ACKNOWLEDGEMENTS

The Association wishes to record its thanks to its members who have given advice in the preparation of these guidelines. The author particularly thanks Carole and Tom Littlechild, whose encouragement, patience and good humour made this publication possible.

EXPLANATORY NOTE ON THE TERMINOLOGY USED IN THIS TEXT

The modes of address for the various groups in this guidance is the same as the adopted in the Act itself and has been used solely in order to make the guidance consistent with the Act in order to avoid any confusion.

That said, the Association wishes to stress that it prefers the modes of address adopted by the United Nations Convention.

©British Association of Social Workers, 1996

Published by The British Association of Social Workers, 16 Kent Street, Birmingham B5 6RD, England

British Library Cataloguing-in-Publication Data.
A catalogue record for this book is available from the British Library

ISBN 1 873878 94 X (paperback)

Cover design by Western Arts, 194 Goswell Road, London EC1V 7DT

Printed 1987
Reprinted and revised 1994
Reprinted and revised 1996

Printed and bound in Great Britain

CONTENTS

Contents

1 INTRODUCTION

THE IMPORTANCE OF THE ACT AND THE CODES OF PRACTICE

The Police and Criminal Evidence Act (PACE) 1984 and the accompanying Codes of Practice, which were revised, updated, and extended in April 1995, represent the first time ever that the powers of the police have been set out in such a detailed manner. The Act is the first occasion when statute has covered so many areas of police activity. Previously, common law had been the main arbiter of police practice.

This book details the changes introduced by the new 1995 Codes, and the relevant changes in the Codes of Practice issued in 1991. Both contain a wealth of changes which clarify or change the previous 1985 Codes. One of the most important changes in the 1995 Code is the inference of guilt a court might draw if a detainee exercises his or her right to silence. One of the other main changes introduced in the 1991 Codes, relating to those acting as appropriate adults, is that solicitors now may not act as appropriate adults. This means that non-relatives such as volunteers, social workers and other professionals, may be called on more often, and has implications for their role, which is discussed in this publication. In addition, guidelines for the police on the role of the appropriate adult will be issued by the Home Office at some point in the future following a Royal Commission on Criminal Justice recommendation emphasising the increasing concern of Government to clarify some of the matters discussed in this book. The last edition of this book, published in 1994, was itself a revision of a previous publication 'Social Work Guidelines to PACE 1984' (BASW 1987). This wholly revised version is aimed at all who may act in this role. This book also sets out the changes that have occurred in the Codes from one revision to the next and, being the only publication to do so, it thereby chronicles the Government's developing view of the appropriate adult role, and effects on practice.

Current issues for the role of the appropriate adult

There may be great variations in how well appropriate adults actually fulfil their role, and how aware they may be of what that role should be. This is true for professionals as well as for others.

It should not be assumed that a solicitor's presence will necessarily ensure that the interests and rights of detainees are upheld. In addition to the solicitor probably having little idea of the particular problems those from the vulnerable groups might have, especially those with mental health problems and learning disabilities, they might not be as effective in this area of work as in others. This is demonstrated in McConville and Hodgson's study (1993), and needs to be something the appropriate adult bears in mind.

Research evidence also shows that the police often do not recognise, or call appropriate adults for those with learning disabilities or mental disorders. As more people in these groups come to live in the community, or remain within it as a result of community care policies, this will become an area of greater concern. People with learning disabilities and mental disorders may not appreciate how their answers will be seen within the criminal justice system, and can be highly suggestible (Gudjonsson, 1992; Clare and Gudjonsson, 1993).

Evidence to the Royal Commission on Criminal Justice in 1993 clearly showed that social workers often did not fulfil the role of appropriate adult satisfactorily; for example, Evans (1993a) found that in 62 per cent of cases where social workers attended, police used 'persuasive' tactics to obtain a confession, despite Code C, 11.3 specifically warning against this. There was only one example of any contribution from professionals in attendance – solicitors were also studied – and Evans (1993b) concluded that 'They may be unaware of, or ignore, the existence of PACE guidance on interviews with vulnerable suspects, or they are unable or unwilling to assert themselves in order to ensure that the police comply with it.'

The appropriate adult can feel deskilled by the alienating environment, and the seemingly unstoppable progress of police-driven events. It is also very much police territory; Simon Holdaway, an ex-police sergeant, described the police station as an 'inner sanctuary... where police are in total control, and social workers are in total control, and social workers (and others) are potential challengers' (Holdaway, 1983).

In addition, Evans (1993b) found that the police often do not explain the role, and may actively try to prevent its being effectively fulfilled. This is in contradiction to the advice in one police manual (*Central Planning and Training Unit Police Manual, 1992,* quoted in Evans, 1993b).

Problems arise in the use of non-professionals as well as professionals as research carried out for the Royal Commission on Criminal Justice demonstrated; while most non-professionals made no contribution at all in the interview 'those that spoke were as likely to be unsupportive of the children in their care... when parents colluded with the police in trying to obtain a confession, they frequently used abusive or appressive techniques reminiscent of the worst police practices' (Evans 1993b). Suggestions for improvement in the arrangements for the provision of appropriate adults are explored by the present author in the *Criminal Law Review* (Littlechild, 1995).

Given these factors any training offered to those who may act as appropriate adults needs to include the following:

* Knowledge of the culture of police forces and investigation methods.

* Consideration of each vulnerable group's particular needs and difficulties, with reference to how they might experience, and react to such methods, particularly in relation to interview techniques.

* How the individual who is acting as an appropriate adult may react to attending in that role; for example, how s/he will react to the police and detainee. Some people react meekly in a police officer's presence; some react aggressively. Some people may have their own prejudices concerning certain detainees. These need to be explored and dealt with, in order to act effectively in the role.

* Use of case studies to practice fulfilling the role and to appreciate the powers and limitations of it.

Duty of local authorities to provide an appropriate adult

Some local authorities do not make it their policy to supply appropriate adults from among their social work or other professional staff. While there is no legislative requirement in relation to other vulnerable groups, juveniles would seem to be covered by the Children's Act 1989, which states that local authorities have a general duty to promote the welfare of children in need in their area (section 17), and Schedule 2(7)(a)(ii), which requires every local authority to take reasonable steps to reduce the need to bring criminal proceedings against children within their area.

In addition, many local authorities based their decision not actively to provide this service as solicitors could undertake it. This is not the case since the 1991 Codes were introduced.

The role of non-relatives acting as appropriate adults

Prior to PACE and the Codes, this whole area was covered in a much less detailed manner, by judges' rules, which concerned themselves with expectations of police behaviour, and had implications, albeit somewhat unclear and unstated, for the role of the social worker called in to assist in a police interview. This role is now more clearly defined under the law and Codes, and there are major implications of which professional workers and their clients, need to be aware. Some professionals may not be called upon to act as an appropriate adult very frequently, so this guidance is set out for both regular and infrequent users. It is a reference work to be used to clarify queries about aspects of the role and of detainees' rights; it is also designed for use as a quick 'refresher' guide when called out at short notice. Chapter 2, the 'Checklist of important points', is particularly for this purpose.

The role of the appropriate adult becomes more important since the implementation of the Criminal Justice and Public Order Act 1994 and the new 1995 Codes of Practice which mean that exercising the right to silence can allow a court to infer guilt. This may place extra pressure and stress on the vulnerable groups to answer inappropriately.

The Codes of Practice represent the first time that guidance has been given in such a formal and codified manner to social workers and others who attend police stations on behalf of people who may be vulnerable when facing the methods of investigation used by the police. They present an opportunity for greater clarity of the role of the appropriate adult. The codes are, however, essentially written for police officers, not social workers and others who act in this role, and it can thus be difficult to ascertain all the aspects and nuances of the role, and to ensure you are representing your duties and your client/detainee effectively. This guide is written to enable the appropriate adult to do just this. Many parents, guardians and others will not have such information on their role available to them and the

British Association of Social Workers hopes that the Home Office will eventually produce brief guidelines for police to give to all who attend as appropriate adults.

This guide, then, will enable social workers, other professionals and lay people to be much clearer and more effective in their role as an appropriate adult. Greater use must be made of this clarity to ensure that the rights of individuals are properly maintained, and that justice is done in terms of the communication between police officers and detainees as Parliament intended when passing the Act and debating the Codes. The appropriate adult has a duty to ensure: adequate understanding between officers and detainees; the recording of the interview is accurate, as this is crucial to all subsequent events; and that the detainee knows his/her rights, and is able to exercise them. In this context, the appropriate adult is not expected to act simply as a observer, but:

> *to advise the person being questioned and to observe whether or not the interview is being conducted properly and fairly,... to facilitate communication with the person being interviewed.*

This role has now been strengthened by the 1991 and 1995 codes as previously this statement appeared in the Notes of Guidance in Code C, 13c; it is now a full part of the Codes, in Code C paragraph 11.16.

The importance of the role was emphasised in the case of Morse and others, in which it was suggested that an appropriate adult who is unable to discharge any or all of the duties attributable to the role is an inappropriate choice, and puts the interviewee at a disadvantage (see *Criminal Law Review*, 195, 1991)

In addition, a new section on appropriate adults in relation to people with a 'mental disorder' or who are 'mentally handicapped' appears in Code C, and sets out this statement again with particular reference to these groups in paragraph 9 of Annex E.

(For a critical appraisal of the role of the appropriate adult, see Littlechild, B. 'The role of the social worker as appropriate adult under PACE 1984: problems, possibilities, and the development of best practice' in *Practice*, 7, (2) 1995.)

It should be noted that these guidelines apply to England and Wales; different legal systems in other areas of Britain mean that this guidance does not necessarily apply in those areas.

USE OF THESE GUIDELINES

This guide covers the main areas of the Act and Codes of Practice with which appropriate adults need to be familiar in order to carry out their duties effectively. It does not cover Code A, concerning police powers of Stop and Search, as the guide is aimed specifically at the rights of detainees and the role of appropriate adult; in pursuance of this, guidance is given on aspects of search of premises arising from such detention; for example, this may lead to the police insisting on gaining entry to Social Services or voluntary agency premises, or a foster home; information is available on this in these guidelines.

The Act and Codes of Practice present a complex set of rights, responsibilities, and guidance which have been included in this guide in a way which sets these duties and powers of the appropriate adult in a chronological order, from the moment the adult is first contacted, through first contact with the client, into the interview situation to its completion and termination of the process. The guide also discusses issues of transfer to local authority care for juveniles, and complaints procedures about police actions.

The guide is set out in a way which provides a full chronological exposition of the local authority's and appropriate adult's duties, and is intended to be read at leisure. It also contains a checklist of main points, again in chronological order, which gives clear reference to the main text. This is intended as a quick reference guide to be used as a reminder of main points and duties in a few minutes, for example, prior to entering the police station. No-one can be expected to carry such details readily in their mind.

Reference is made in the text to the paragraphs and sections of the Act and Codes, as it can be important to have ready access to the exact wording and status of each source. Terms such as 'appropriate adult' and 'vulnerable person' are fully defined in the text.

It is important to remember that the Codes must be readily available, at all police stations designated to hold detainees, to whoever wishes to consult them, whenever they wish to do so (Codes of Practice, Code

C, Paragraph 1.2). In addition, a new requirement in the 1991 Code that was retained 1995 was that a poster should be displayed prominently so that detainees will be made aware of their right to legal advice in the charging area of every police station (Codes of Practice, Code C, Paragraph 6.3); so that they should be reminded that this will be free (Codes of Practice, Code C, Paragraphs 11.2, 15.3, and Code D, Paragraphs 2.15(ii) and 5.2, concerning identification of suspects). The posters about legal advice should be in languages other than English where this is likely to be helpful (Codes of Practice, Code C, Note of Guidance 6H). There seems to be no duty on the police, however, to make a copy of the Act available.

References to the Act and Codes in the text take the following form:

- Codes of Practice, Code C, Paragraph 1.1, for example, translates to (COP, C, 1.1)

- Codes of Practice, Code C, Note of Guidance 11B, for example, translates to (COP, C, NOG, 11B)

- Section 38(3) Police and Criminal Evidence Act 1984, for example, translates to (PACE, s. 38(3))

There have been two revisions of the Codes, in 1991 and 1995. Where changes are referred to from the 1991 Codes they have been retained in the 1995 revision.

LEGAL STATUS OF THE CODES

Unlike the Act itself, the Codes of Practice do not have the weight of law; they were required to be produced by the statute itself (PACE, s. 66). A breach of the Codes could lead to disciplinary action against police officers, but the Codes themselves are not enforceable in any immediate way. Therefore, if the appropriate adult is to perform her/his role correctly, by using this guide the Codes and the Act, s/he must ensure proper representations are made to the right person at the right time, and that these are recorded fully at the police station in the correct way. This guide will enable you to do this. These records will then be of vital importance in subsequent proceedings to ensure that justice is done; for example, a court may rule a statement or confession inadmissible if parts of the Codes were breached, and the detained person's solicitor can show this from the 'custody record' and any comments made on it. The juveniles accused of the murder of P.C. Keith Blakelock in the Broadwater Farm disturbances were in part found not guilty because of substantial breaches of the Codes in relation to conditions of detention and the police attitude to solicitors and to the social worker acting as appropriate adult, and the effect this had on gaining evidence.

It is the existence of the law and the Codes of Practice, and the very presence of the appropriate adult that safeguard the detainee's rights, if the appropriate adult knows their role, and uses this knowledge well. Most of the appropriate adult's role is now spelt out in the full Codes, but not in the Act itself.

The Notes of Guidance have a more tenuous status; they are 'not provisions of this Code, but are guidance to police officers and others about its application and interpretation', but the 'Provisions in the annexes of this code are (full) provisions of this Code' (COP, C, 1.3).

All the provisions in the original Codes and Notes of Guidance were subject to four drafts, each involving extensive consultations. The revised Codes issued in 1991 and 1995 attempted to address issues raised by various concerned groups, and led to some significant changes, as detailed in this guide. It seems clear, then, that the Codes were very carefully prepared under the aegis of Parliament, and are meant to be observed closely, and treated seriously.

CHANGES FROM THE FIRST EDITION OF THE CODES IN THE SECOND EDITION (1991) CODES OF PRACTICE AND THE CRIMINAL JUSTICE ACT 1991: AREAS OF PARTICULAR RELEVANCE TO APPROPRIATE ADULTS

The main changes affecting the appropriate adult fully set out in this guide are:

- A solicitor attending in a professional capacity should not act as an appropriate adult.

- A new set of provisions is set out for 'mentally disordered' people (formerly referred to in the first edition of the Codes as 'mentally ill' people) and 'mentally handicapped' people. 'Mentally disordered' people now have greater safeguards in relation to section 136 of the Mental Health Act 1983.

- The statement about the role of the appropriate adult is now contained in the full Codes, and not just in the Notes of Guidance.

- The right to free legal advice has now to be clearly set out in posters in locally appropriate languages and stated explicitly to detainees.

- It is more difficult for police to exclude solicitors from interviews.

- In addition to these new provisions, the Criminal Justice Act 1991 sets out new criteria for the decision about transfer to local authority care.

CHANGES IN THE THIRD EDITION (1995) FROM THE SECOND EDITION (1991) CODES OF PRACTICE AND THE CRIMINAL JUSTICE AND PUBLIC ORDER ACT 1994

A set of updated Codes was published by the Home Office in April 1995 to take effect from midnight on 9 April.

There are some minor changes which result from a general review of procedures, and more major changes arising from the enactment of the Criminal Justice and Public Order Act 1994, sections 36 and 37, which relate to a fundamental change in English law. This change means that a court can draw inference of guilt if a suspect chooses to exercise her/his right to silence, which in turn has led to a change in the caution referred to in the codes.

The main changes in the 1995 Codes which the appropriate adult needs to have an awareness of are as follows:

1 A new section 10.4A in the 1995 has been inserted, changing the nature of the caution, which will now be in the following form: 'You do not have to say anything. But it may harm your defence if you do not mention when questioned something which you later rely on in court. Anything you say may be given in evidence.' Minor deviations do not constitute a breach of this requirement provided that the sense of the caution is preserved.

The revised section 10.4 includes a new statement to confirm that the caution must make clear to the detainee the effects of silence.

The appropriate adult should ensure that the detainee understands what this means, and that s/he knows s/he can discuss any concerns at any time with the appropriate adult, and that the appropriate adult can call a solicitor at any time if s/he thinks this is necessary (COP, C, 3.13).

New sections 10.5A and B relate to special warnings about exercising the right to silence.

2   A revised section 1.7 states that in relation to a juvenile who is 'in care' this term relates to all cases in which a juvenile is 'looked after' by a local authority under the terms of the Children Act 1989.

3   A new section 1.1A in the 1995 Codes states that a custody officer is required to perform the functions specified in the role as soon as is practicable, and reasons must be recorded in the custody record; delays which are justifiable, and where all reasonable steps have been taken to prevent them, will not be deemed to breach the Codes. New Note of Guidance 1H gives examples of where delay might be justifiable, e.g. difficulties in contacting an appropriate adult, solicitor or interpreter.

4   The 1995 Code states that while the Code's provisions cover those taken to police stations under section 135 or 136 of the Mental Health Act 1983, reviews of detention do not apply to these groups (COP, C, 1.10).

5   A new section 1.12 sets out certain groups not covered by the Code, which does not affect the appropriate adult's role.

6   Note of Guidance 1C is changed to include people other than parents or guardians who should be excluded as appropriate adults where they are the victim or suspected of being involved in the offence being investigated. Neither are witnesses now to be used.

7   A new Note of Guidance 1EE makes it clear that the detainee can meet with the solicitor in private, excluding the appropriate adult, if s/he wishes.

8   A new Note of Guidance 1I states that it is important for the custody officer to record any reasons for waiving the right to see a solicitor, under section 6 of Code C.

9   Audio or video recordings made in the custody area do not form part of the custody record (COP, C, 2.1). If video is used, prominent notices to this effect must be displayed. They will not be switched off at the request of the detainee (COP, C, 3.5A).

10 A solicitor or appropriate adult must be permitted to consult the custody record of a person detained as soon as practicable after their arrival at the police station (COP, C, 2.4).

11 All entries into the custody record must be timed and dated, including on computers, when the operator must enter his/her identification number (COP, C, 2.6).

12 The custody officer should not invite comment from the detainee on the arresting officer's account, or on a decision to detain him/her (COP, C, 3.4).

13 The detainee must sign the custody record to confirm his/her decision to call legal advice or not, and that her/his rights have been given verbally and in writing. This must be done on the arrival of the appropriate adult, whether done previously or not (COP, C, 3.2, 3.5 and 3.11).

14 COP, C, 6.6(d) allows an interview to continue if a detainee has asked for legal advice, later changes her/his mind, and an Inspector or above agrees.

15 Police officers cannot advise on firms of solicitors (NOG, 6B).

16 Detainees must be told when their solicitor arrives, unless Annex B applies (COP, C, 6.15).

17 The 1994 Criminal Justice and Public Order Act reduces from 15 to 12 the age at which a juvenile can be detained under PACE s.38(b).

18 In the case of a mentally handicapped or mentally disordered person, particular care must be taken when deciding whether to use handcuffs (COP, C, 8.2).

19 An appropriate adult or solicitor may request delay or interruption of the 8-hour rest period (COP, C, 12.2).

20 A new Note 12C states that meal breaks should normally last at least 45 minutes, and shorter breaks after 2 hours should last at least 15 minutes; if these are delayed in accordance with paragraph 12.7, a longer break should then be provided. If there is a short interview, and a subsequent short interview is contemplated, the length of the break may be reduced to avoid any of the consequences set out in paragraphs 12.7(i) to (iii).

21 A new paragraph 11.1A referring to the exclusion of section 7 of the Road Traffic Act from the requirement for interviews to be carried out under caution.

22 Reasons for police being able to interview in the absence of an interpreter, someone who has hearing or speech disabilities (COP, C, 13.5), or where the parent or guardian attending as an appropriate adult is so disabled (COP, C, 13.6), are set out in paragraph 11.1 as well as Annex C.

23 Reviews of detention: the review officer shall not put questions about the alleged offence, or any comments the detainee makes about any decision to detain him/her further; this is a new COP, C, 15.2A provision.

24 The review officer must remind the detainee of his/her right to free legal advice under revised paragraph 6.5, which states it must be made clear that the detainee can consult a solicitor over the telephone, and that if s/he refuses, s/he will be asked why, and the response, if any, recorded.

25 When a detainee is charged, or informed that s/he may be prosecuted for an offence, s/he will be cautioned in the following terms: 'You do not have to say anything. But it may harm your defence if you do not mention now something which you later rely on in court. Anything you do say may be given in evidence.' (COP, C, 16.2).

26 The notice of charge will contain the same warning as set out in 25 above, and will be given to the appropriate adult (COP, C, 16.3).

27 If a person is charged or informed that s/he may be prosecuted for an offence, and a police officer wishes to bring to the notice of that person any written statement made by another person or the content of an interview with another person, the officer will hand a true copy of this to the detainee, but will say or do nothing to invite a reply concerning this, except to say that the detainee does not have to say anything, but anything s/he does say may be used in evidence, and to remind him/her of the right to free legal advice. If the detainee is from one of the vulnerable groups, the copy will also be given to the appropriate adult (COP,C, 16.4).

28 A revised section COP, C, NOG ID, states that 'if a juvenile admits an offence to or in the presence of a social worker other than during the time that the social worker is acting as the appropriate adult for that juvenile, another social worker should be the appropriate adult in the interest of fairness.' Previously, the 1991 codes stated that the social worker should withdraw if a child in care admits an offence.

REFERENCES

Central Planning and Training Unit Police Manual, 1992, quoted in Evans (1993b).

Clare, I.C.H. and Gudjonsson, G.H. (1993), 'Interrogative suggestibility, confabulation and acquiescence in people with mild learning disabilities (mental handicap): Implications for reliability during police interrogations,' *British Journal of Clinical Psychology*, 32: 295-301.

Evans, R. (1993a) Royal Commission on Criminal Justice, Research Study 8, *'The Conduct of Police Interviews with Juveniles'* London: HMSO (1993b) 'Getting things taped', *Community Care*, 18 November.

Gudjonsson, G. (1992) 'The psychology of false confessions and ways to improve the system', *Expert Evidence*, August.

Gudjonsson, G. *et al.*, (1993) *Royal Commission on Criminal Justice Research Study 12*, London: HMSO.

Holdaway, S. (1983) *'Inside the British Police'*. Oxford: Blackwell.

Littlechild, B. (1995) 'Re-assessing the role of the appropriate adult', *Criminal Law Review*, July.

McConville, M. and Hodgson, J. (1993) *Royal Commission on Criminal Justice Research Study 16, London: HMSO.*

Home Office (1984) *Police and Criminal Evidence Act 1984*. London: HMSO.

Home Office (1985) *Police and Criminal Evidence Act 1984 (s.66) Codes of Practice* First edition London: HMSO.

Home Office (1988) *Police and Criminal Evidence Act 1984 (s.60(1)(a)): Code of Practice (E) on tape recording*. London: HMSO.

Home Office (1991) Police and Criminal Evidence Act 1984 (s.66): Codes of Practice, 2nd edition. London: HMSO.

Home Office (1995) *Police and Criminal Evidence Act 1984 (s.60(1)(a) and s. 66): Codes of Practice* 3rd edition. London: HMSO.

Viscount Runciman, CBE, FBA (1993) *'Royal Commission on Criminal Justice Report'*. London: HMSO

2 CHECKLIST OF IMPORTANT POINTS

This checklist is intended to act as a resume of the areas covered in the guide, and as a quick reference guide to the appropriate adult's duties, and the rights of the detainee. The page numbers quoted refer the reader to the pages on which a full exposition of these points is set out.

1 INTRODUCTION

The importance of the Act and the codes of practice

- The Act and Codes represent the first time police powers and duties have been so clearly defined (page 1).

- The Act and Codes provide clear guidance for appropriate adults about their role when they are called on to act when the Act and Codes have been re-formulated for their use as in this book (pages 6, 7).

- The local authority's duties concerning the provision of appropriate adults are clearer for juveniles than it is for the other 'vulnerable groups' (page 3).

Legal status of the Codes

- The Codes have to be available to whoever wishes to consult them at any time in a police station which is authorised to hold detainees (page 6).

- The Codes do not have the status of law, but breaches of them can be taken into account in subsequent court hearings, and can lead to disciplinary action within the police force (page 7).

- The Notes of Guidance have less status in any proceedings than the full Codes (page 8).

- The third edition of the Codes (1995), the Criminal Justice Act 1991 and the Criminal Justice and Public Order Act 1994 set out new requirements which affect the role of the social worker and other non-relatives acting as appropriate adult (page 9).

2   BEFORE GOING TO THE POLICE STATION

The vulnerable groups under the Codes of Practice

- These groups, and the police duty to recognise them, are discussed on page 31. The groups non-relatives are most likely to be involved with are juveniles, mentally disordered people, and mentally handicapped people. (Terms used are those used in the Codes of Practice).

- The custody officer should carry out her/his duties as soon as practicable (page 34).

- Appropriate adults, usually Approved Social Workers under the Mental Health Act 1983, will attend for people who are held by police under section 136 of the Mental Health Act 1983 (pages 31, 38). The review of detention requirements do not apply to these groups.

- Details of the Codes' provisions concerning a detainee being held incommunicado, and/or without access to a solicitor, are set out in Annex B and Annex C (pages 34, 39 and 45).

- An appropriate adult can be present when a solicitor is prevented from attending under Annex B. In this instance, it is vital that the appropriate adult gives the detainee proper advice, bearing in mind that the social worker cannot, and is not there to, take on the full role of legal adviser. A solicitor being excluded from an interview is now less likely under the new 1991 and 1995 Codes, but it is still possible (page 46).

When should an appropriate adult or interpreter be called?

This should be done as soon as practicable (page 34).

Who is an appropriate adult?

- The different categories of persons eligible to be called upon for different vulnerable groups are listed on pages 36–40.

- The role of the appropriate adult is strengthened by full inclusion of the role in the Codes, as is the role of the Approved Social Worker in relation to detainees subject to section 136 of the Mental Health Act (page 38).

Cautionary note for non-relatives called on to act as an appropriate adult

- Ensure that all efforts have been made to contact the parents or guardians to secure their attendance. Any non-relative should attempt this themselves should the police fail to do so. If the police did not make efforts to contact parents or guardians prior to contacting a social worker or other non-relative (where the detainee is not a juvenile accommodated by the local authority) to act as an appropriate adult or were slow in contacting any of these people before securing their attendance, this should be reported to the custody officer. It should also be reported to the appropriate manager in the professional's agency, where appropriate, for the matter to be taken up with the police. If any of these situations apply, inform the detainee's solicitor.

- Situations where a detainee will have someone else called in preference to a parent or guardian are where the latter is:
  (a)   suspected of involvement in the offence;
  (b)   the victim;
  (c)   involved in the investigation or has received admissions;
  (d)   estranged from the juvenile and the juvenile objects to his/her presence (page 36).

- A solicitor or a lay visitor acting in that capacity and an appropriate adult should not be the same person (page 36).

- The calling of a solicitor by someone from one of the vulnerable groups should not be delayed until the appropriate adult arrives, if this is asked for by the detainee (page 44).

- The custody officer must ensure the detainee and appropriate adult are reminded of their right to call free legal advice.

- The detainee has the right to see his/her solicitor in private away from the appropriate adult.

3   AT THE POLICE STATION

The appropriate adult at the police station and their role in calling for legal advice

- Make further checks that relatives are still unavailable, or are unwilling to attend.

- Ensure that you see the detainee on your own to fully explain your role, and the limits of confidentiality. The detainee can also see the solicitor in private away from the appropriate adult. You have the right to see the detainee on your own. It is important to make the distinction between your role and the solicitor's role, and that if the detainee admits guilt to you, another appropriate adult will have to be called. Ensure that you explain your role fully to the detainee on your own, before you do anything else (pages 54–58).

- Ensure that the detainee is given orally and in writing a list of his/her rights in your presence (page 49). This has to take place even if the police have previously done this prior to your arrival. The detainee should be told that they can take legal advice over the telephone. If s/he still refuses, reasons for this will be recorded (page 45, 49).

- Of particular importance is that the detainee is fully aware that s/he can call a solicitor at any stage during their detention even if they have chosen not to earlier, absolutely free of charge (page 44). The appropriate adult can also choose to do this at any stage on her/his own initiative if s/he believes it necessary. This is to protect the rights of a vulnerable person; if s/he requests legal advice police should act on this straight away and not wait for the appropriate adult. The solicitor could be a non-accredited or probationary representative at the police's discretion. The police should not advise on any particular firm of solicitors.

- The police can only require a detainee to continue being questioned in very particular circumstances while awaiting the attendance of the solicitor or where s/he has asked for legal advice and later declines it, and then only if an inspector agrees (page 45).

- The other rights of the detainee are to see the Codes of Practice at any time, see the custody record at the end of their detention, or ask to see it up to one year afterwards (page 64).

- Check that the proper caution has been given, and that the detainee understands it and its implications; this includes being told of her/his right to remain silent, but that if s/he chooses to exercise this right, the court might subsequently infer guilt from this (pages 50–53).

- Check who the custody officer is; there must be one appointed when a person is detained. S/he is vital to subsequent events, as the custody officer is personally responsible for ensuring the rights of the detainee are upheld, as set out in the Act and Codes of Practice. If you have issues or complaints that you have raised with the interviewing officer which you believe have not been satisfactorily dealt with, you will need to request to see the custody officer, who cannot refuse to see you (page 61).

• Check that no 'informal statements' have been made prior to your arrival, and what has been talked about between the police and the detainee (page 43).

• Check the time at which the person was detained, the grounds for detention, and that the detainee is fully aware of these grounds.

• The detainee must be told when their solicitor arrives at the station (page 47).

The role of the appropriate adult in the interview

• It is possible that the appropriate adult could be questioned in subsequent court hearings about an interview in which s/he has been involved (page 57).

• Make sure that the detainee understands what is happening, and that s/he understands the questions asked, and possible interpretations of the answers (page 57).

• Make sure that there is no 'oppression' or offensive remarks used by the interviewing officers, or that there are any signs of neglect or abuse (page 57).

• The appropriate adult's role is defined as being to facilitate communication between the detainee and the police and, most importantly, to ensure that the interview is being conducted fairly (pages 58, 59).

• Keep notes of what happens in the interview (page 61).

• Ensure that if there are breaks in the interview that the interviewing officer reiterates the right of the detainee to free legal advice if s/he has not already availed her/himself of this opportunity (page 58).

• If there are irregularities which appear to be in breach of the Act or Codes, the appropriate adult has a duty to make representations to the custody officer (page 61), or the review officer, if it concerns the period of detention (page 68).

- You may wish to call a solicitor if you receive an unsatisfactory response. Keep notes of this as they may be needed later (page 62).

- The rights of the detainee and the appropriate adult's role in delaying or interrupting the 8-hour rest period, are set out on pages 60 and 61. These include the need to take special care in using handcuffs on 'mentally handicapped' or 'mentally disordered' detainees.

- A solicitor or appropriate adult can be ordered to leave an interview. If an appropriate adult is ordered to leave, a further appropriate adult must be found (page 62).

Interview and custody records

- The appropriate adult has a duty to ensure that these are accurate, and will be given the opportunity to read and sign the interview record, or any other written statement taken down by a police officer. Again, if there are queries, or issues to be raised, these require the attendance of the custody officer (page 63).

- The appropriate adult and solicitor must be allowed to examine the custody record as soon as practicable upon arrival. S/he should ask to examine the custody record before leaving the situation if there is a query about any aspect of the person's detention. This record must state when and why decisions were made by the police and entries timed and dated. Copies of it must be made available as soon as possible after the detention, at the request of the detainee, his/her solicitor, or (as from 1991) the appropriate adult. These people can request a copy of the custody record up to 12 months after the detainee's release (page 64, 65).

Charging and release of detained persons

- The detainee should be charged, and questioning cease, as soon as there is enough evidence to do this (page 64).

- The appropriate adult should be present when the detainee is charged (page 64).

- The detainee is then free to leave after charge unless one of the criteria set out on pages 65 and 66 applies. Special criteria concerning transfer of a juvenile to local authority accommodation apply (pages 66 and 68).

Continued detention before charge

- The appropriate adult will need to ensure that proper reviews of detention take place at the designated times, which are laid out fully in the Act. The first review takes place 6 hours after the start of the detention (pages 68 and 71). This does not apply to those detained under s.135 or s.136 of the Mental Health Act 1983.

- Time limits for detention before someone is brought to court is a complex process to calculate. Detailed references to the Act are given on page 71.

- Detention without charge can be for up to 36 hours before the detainee is brought before a court, or 48 hours if someone is detained under the Prevention of Terrorism legislation (page 71).

- Reviews can only be postponed for specific reasons (page 69).

- The detainee and his/her solicitor can make representations concerning further detention at these reviews; the appropriate adult may also do this (page 70).

Giving consent to police actions

- The above actions normally require the appropriate adult's consent as well as that of the detainee, though this can be overridden by the police. If the detainee is a juvenile, the consent of her/his parent or guardian is required in addition to that of the juvenile, unless the juvenile is under 14, when the consent of the parent or guardian is sufficient in itself. Particular care should be taken by non-relatives who act as appropriate adults that they do not agree to certain police actions, as only parents or guardians can give such consent. Who may give consent to what is set out on page 72.

- Strip searches and non-intimate searches do not necessarily require this consent (page 78).

- Particular details concerning intimate and non-intimate body samples are set out on pages 80 and 81.

- If appropriate consent is withheld without "good cause" over the taking of an intimate body sample, those sitting in judgement in subsequent court hearings may draw certain conclusions from this (page 81).

Identity parades, confrontation by a witness, group identifications and video films

- An appropriate adult finding her/himself in a situation where this may occur should always involve or consult a solicitor and parents or guardians, even if they have refused to attend earlier, or were unable to (page 74).

- Where the detainee is mentally handicapped, or is mentally disordered, her/his consent is only valid if given in the presence of the appropriate adult. In the case of a juvenile, the consent of the parent or guardian is required as well as that of the juvenile, unless s/he is under 14 (COP, D, 1.11) (page 73).

- The suspect must be given a written notice stating the terms of the parade or identification, and that s/he may refuse, but this may lead to a confrontation by a witness, or a group identification, and a refusal may be given in evidence in any subsequent trial, and identification take place in court (page 74).

- The suspect must be given a reasonable opportunity to have a solicitor present (page 74).

- Once the parade is formed, or a confrontation by a witness arranged, subsequent events have to be witnessed by an interpreter, solicitor, friend or appropriate adult, unless, as in the case of a witness confrontation, this will cause unreasonable delay. If an informal parade is planned a solicitor should be called (page 74).

Photographs of the detainee (and computer images)

- 'Appropriate consent' from the appropriate adult attending has to be given in writing for juveniles, mentally disordered people and mentally handicapped people, or those mentally incapable of understanding the process. In the case of juveniles, a social worker or other professional acting as the appropriate adult cannot give consent. This will have to be obtained by the police from parents or guardians (pages 74, 75).

- This consent can only be waived in certain circumstances (page 75). This may mean taking someone to the police station for the photograph to be taken if they have been convicted of a recordable offence.

- Suspects must be told of their right to see the destruction of negatives, or to receive a copy of a certificate confirming their destruction, if s/he is cleared of the offence, or charges are not brought. Photographs may be kept if the detainee agrees to a caution. Force may not be used by the police to take photographs (page 75).

Fingerprinting and palmprinting of the detainee

- Fingerprints or palmprints may be taken by the police with the use of 'reasonable' force, even if the consent of the detainee and appropriate adult is unforthcoming. In the case of a juvenile, a social worker can only give consent if the young person is being accommodated under a care order by his/her local authority or voluntary organisation; otherwise, such consent can only come from parents or guardians. Ten years is the minimum age for police to take fingerprints forcibly (page 76).

- The circumstances in which fingerprints can be taken forcibly are set out on page 76.

- These include requiring a person to attend the police station at some point after s/he has been charged or reported for a recordable offence, or if s/he has been convicted of a recordable offence (page 77).

- The same conditions for witnessing or receiving a certificate concerning destruction of fingerprints exist as for photographs (page 75).

Strip searches, intimate and non-intimate body searches, and body samples

- Strip searches and non-intimate body searches do not require the detainee's or the appropriate adult's consent, and can be carried out under PACE, or under sections 135 or 136 on people detained under the Mental Health Act 1983 (page 77).

- Strip searches may only be carried out by an officer of the same sex, in order to remove an article the detainee is not allowed to keep, and

23

no person of the opposite sex who is not a nurse or medical practitioner shall be present (page 78).

- Intimate body searches have to be authorised by an officer of the rank of at least superintendent, and be for the removal of certain Class A concealed drugs or weapons. Intimate searches for weapons may be carried out at the police station, or at a hospital, surgery or other medical premises; a search for Class A drugs may only take place at a hospital, surgery or other medical premises (page 79).

- An intimate body search for drugs has to be carried out by a suitably qualified person i.e. a nurse or a doctor. A search for a weapon should always be made by a medically qualified person unless a superintendent deems it impractical, when it should be carried out by a constable of the same sex (page 79).

- The appropriate adult must be present at the intimate search of a juvenile, or a mentally disordered or mentally handicapped person (unless a juvenile states that s/he wishes the appropriate adult not to be present, in the latter's presence). In any event, no person of the opposite sex may be present unless the detainee particularly requests the presence of a specific adult of the opposite sex, who is readily available. If the detainee wishes for an appropriate adult to remain, a person of the same sex will need to be contacted to attend, if the initial adult is not of the same sex unless the detainee particularly requests his/her presence (page 79).

- The taking of intimate or non-intimate body samples requires appropriate consent. Definitions and procedures are set out on pages 80 and 81.

4   TAPE RECORDING OF INTERVIEWS

When tape recording will be used

- All parts of all interviews will be tape recorded (page 84) except where someone is detained under the Prevention of Terrorism Act, or other special circumstances (pages 84 and 85).

The arrangements for the interview

- Information to be given to the detainee (page 85).

Objections and complaints by the detainee

• Any objections should be recorded on the tape, but the officer can continue the tape recording (page 86).

• Any complaint about treatment must be investigated (page 86).

Breaks in the interview

• Reasons for breaks in the recording must be stated on the tape (page 87).

• If proceedings follow, a written record of the interview will be made (page 87).

Recording and sealing of the master tapes

• Master tapes are sealed in the presence of the detainee, and can only be opened by the Crown Procecution Service (page 88).

The detainee will have access to a working tape (pages 88 and 89).

The appropriate adult's role

• To ensure fair interview techniques are taking place, and facilitate communication (page 88).

5 ISSUES OF RELEASE OF JUVENILES AFTER CHARGE AND TRANSFER TO LOCAL AUTHORITY CARE

Charging and releasing

• Once a person is charged, s/he must be released with or without bail to appear in court except in certain circumstances as outlined on page 93.

• If a formal caution is considered by the police, ensure that the police's own guidelines for giving cautions are followed; these are set out on page 91. It is important not to consider the issuing of a caution lightly as it will be recorded as an offence on the young person's police record (page 91).

• A juvenile may be detained after charge if the police believe s/he ought to be so detained in her/his best interests (page 92).

The police duty to inform and consult the local authority

- The police have a duty to inform and consult the local authority concerning the transfer into their care of a juvenile who is charged and subsequently detained (page 92).

- If the police decide that transfer to local authority care is not practicable, or does not fall within section 38(6) of PACE as amended by the Criminal Justice Act 1991, they must produce a certificate which has to be produced in court on the first occasion on which the juvenile is presented there (page 93).

- The age at which a young person may be detained under s.38(b) of the Act has been lowered to 12.

The duty of the local authority

- DHSS (as it was when issued) guidance says that local authorities should ensure that adequate arrangements are available for social services departments to be contacted at all times to ensure an arrested and detained juvenile can be passed into their care (page 94).

- Local authorities must ensure that an arrested juvenile placed in their care must have available advice and assistance as may be appropriate in the circumstances. They must have regard to all the rights of the young person under the Codes of Practice (page 95).

- Social services departments will wish to ensure that all who will be involved in the care of the young person have access to clear guidelines concerning the young person's rights, and the local authority duty towards them. This may mean field- workers, residential workers, and foster parents (page 95).

Secure accommodation

- Local authorities may use secure accommodation for young people placed in their care under the Act without having to comply with the secure accommodation regulations outlined in the Children Act 1989 (page 95).

Producing the young person in court

- The social services department has a duty to produce the young person at the subsequent court hearing, and to ensure that suitable arrangements are made to escort the young person to the court (page 96).

Child care duties of a social worker acting as an appropriate adult

- The appropriate adult attending will need to have an awareness of the different roles to be carried out, as it may be that the 'appropriate adult' role gives way to a more general child care role. The appropriate adult attending will want to ensure that if the young person's circumstances look as though this may be the case, they should make this known to the young person before events get under way so that everyone understands the situation. If there is any doubt about the transfer of care to a local authority, the social worker will want to check in these guidelines the legality of such transfers, and to ascertain whether work with the young person and the family means that release from a police station can take place without a substitute care episode resulting (page 96).

6 THE SEARCHING OF RESIDENTIAL HOMES, DAY CENTRES AND OTHER PREMISES BY THE POLICE

Access to premises

- Police may only search an establishment in certain prescribed circumstances. Staff and managers of such an establishment will need to be familiar with the provisions of the Act in order to protect the legal rights of the whole of the user group. This is of particular importance to those working in establishments serving young people, mentally handicapped, mentally disordered people, and to foster-parents (page 99).

- The police may enter establishments by way of a warrant signed by a J P, produced to the person in charge of the establishment. This is valid on one occasion only within one month of date of issue (page 99).

- Access without a warrant is only possible in certain prescribed circumstances set out on page 100, or where the person in charge of the establishment at the time grants entry. The person in charge will want to consider carefully reasons for entry in such circumstances, and be aware of what limits they should put on the police search and the possible effect on other residents or users of the establishment (page 101).

Seizure of material on the premises

- This is of vital importance to those who find themselves in charge of the establishment and when a search is with or without a warrant. A constable can seize anything he or she believes has been obtained in consequence of the commission of an offence, or may be evidence of an offence which he or she believes has been committed. Computer records are included under this section unless they contain 'excluded material'. This has important implications for where the officer is allowed to search, and the limits on this are set out on page 102.

Material excluded from seizure under a general search

- Knowledge of such excluded materials which the police may not seize is important for the person in charge of an establishment at any particular time. Certain documents, including social work records are excluded from a constable's power of seizure, unless a special warrant is issued by a Circuit Judge. The definition of such material as is excluded is given on page 103.

Search under Schedule 1 of the Act or the Prevention of Terrorism (Temporary Provisions) Act 1989 for confidential material

- Even if such a search does lawfully take place, 'items subject to legal privilege' are in no circumstances available to the police; this material is communication between a client and his/her solicitor. If the police do search files as this material should be removed prior to the search (page 104).

7 COMPLAINTS AGAINST POLICE BEHAVIOUR: PART IX OF THE ACT

- A new complaints procedure was introduced by the 1984 PACE Act, and any member of the public including a social worker or other non-relative may make a complaint on behalf of a detainee with the latter's written permission. As a matter of good practice any complaint should come from the aggrieved party where this is possible (page 105).

• The amount of support which a social worker will give in any particular circumstance will depend on the individual situation. At the very least, an appropriate adult should advise the person to contact a solicitor or Citizen's Advice Bureau, and explain the manner in which a complaint will be dealt with (page 105).

• Complaints should be addressed to the Chief Constable of the police force concerned (page 105).

• Where complaints are found to be unjustified, the police can sue a complainant (page 105).

• If a complaint is upheld, this does not necessarily invalidate evidence obtained during the course of the investigation in court. The extent to which material could be inadmissible would have to be judged by the magistrates or judge in the light of the facts from the defence solicitor (page 105).

3 BEFORE GOING TO THE POLICE STATION

THE VULNERABLE GROUPS UNDER THE CODES OF PRACTICE

These are defined in the Codes of Practice, section C, paragraphs 1.4 to 1.6:

- mentally disordered people (the 1991 Codes introduced to this category those detained under the Mental Health Act 1983, sections 135 and 136, as well as those detained under PACE);

- people with mental handicaps;

- juveniles.

These groups above have to receive the services of an appropriate adult. The following groups, while meriting safeguards, are not afforded the services of a full appropriate adult role:

- those who are blind or who are seriously visually handicapped;

- those unable to read;

- those unable to speak or who have difficulty orally because of speech impediment;

- those who are deaf.

How do the police recognise these groups?

Mentally disordered and mentally handicapped people

> *If an officer has any suspicion, or is told in good faith, that a person of any age may be mentally disordered or mentally handicapped, or mentally incapable of understanding the significance of questions put to him or his replies, then that person shall be treated as a mentally disordered or mentally handicapped person for the purposes of this Code. (COP, C, 1.4)*

31

Note 1G of Code C states that 'the generic term "mental disorder" is used throughout this Code. "Mental disorder" is defined by the Mental Health Act 1983 as "mental illness, arrested or incomplete development of mind, psychopathic disorder and any other disorder or disability of mind".' It should be noted that 'mental disorder' is different to 'mental handicap' although the two forms are dealt with similarly throughout this code. There is no further definition of 'mental handicap', though, as the Mental Health Act 1983 is referred to, it would seem that the definition of mental handicap in that Act could be used. A wider definition is implied in the Code's reference.

The new 1991 Codes are more clear concerning when a doctor and an Approved Social Worker should be called (see page 38) though this will not apply to all who appear to be 'mentally disordered', and in this latter situation, and for those who appear to be 'mentally handicapped', there would seem to be a great deal of discretion in how the police define such groups. Statements from others, or appearances are enough. This would seem to err on the right side of caution where someone may be in need of the support and advice an appropriate adult should be able to give.

Juveniles

'If anyone appears to be under the age of 17 then he shall be treated as a juvenile for the purposes of this code in the absence of clear evidence to show that he is older.' (COP, C, 1.5). This again seems to err on the side of caution and in favour of ensuring proper safeguards for young people.

'Juveniles may only be interviewed at their places of education in exceptional circumstances and then only when the principal or his nominee agrees.' (COP, C, 11.15). (See also page 37 concerning those who can act as an appropriate adult in these circumstances.)

Those who are blind, seriously visually handicapped, deaf, unable to speak or have difficulty orally because of a speech impediment

A detainee only has to 'appear to be' in one of these categories to be treated as such, in the absence of clear evidence to the contrary (COP, C, 1.6). Citizens of independent Commonwealth countries or foreign nationals do not require an appropriate adult, but may need an interpreter, and have a right to contact their embassy at any time (COP, C, 7); and Note of Guidance 7A states that this right 'may not be interfered with even though Annex B' (see page 45) applies.

If the detainee appears to be deaf or there is doubt about her/his hearing or speaking ability or ability to understand English, and the custody officer cannot establish effective communication, the custody officer must call an interpreter as soon as possible. The interpreter must then ensure the detainee knows her/his rights. The detainee should be made aware by all practicable steps that the interpreter will be provided at the public expense (COP, C, 13.8). Please refer to paragraphs 13.1 to 13.11 of Code C for specific guidance on the interpreter's role for those who are deaf, unable to speak or who have difficulty orally because of a speech impediment, or who have difficulty communicating in English.

An interpreter should be called in these instances:

(a) *When the detainee has difficulty in understanding English and the interviewing officer cannot himself speak the person's language; and if the detainee requests it (COP, C, 13.2)*

(b) *When the detainee appears to be 'deaf or speech handicapped', then s/he should not be interviewed in the absence of an interpreter unless s/he agrees in writing to being interviewed without one. In addition, if the detainee is a juvenile, and the parent or guardian who is acting as appropriate adult appears to fall into this category, an interpreter should be called, 'unless s/he agrees in writing that the interview should proceed without one.' (COP, C, 13.6)*

In both (a) and (b) above, questioning can continue without an interpreter if Annex C applies (see page 35).

The role of the interpreter

The interpreter should 'make a note of the interview at the time in the language of the person being interviewed for use in the event of his being called to give evidence.' The interpreter shall be given sufficient time to 'make a note of each question and answer after each has been put or given and interpreted. The person shall be given an opportunity to read it or have it read to him and sign it as accurate or to indicate the respects in which he considers it inaccurate. If the interview is tape recorded, the arrangements set out in Code E apply.' (see Chapter 5)

(COP, C, 13.3). In the case of a person making a statement in a language other than English:

(a) *The interpreter shall take down the statement in the language in which it is made;*

(b) *The person making the statement shall be invited to sign and*

(c) *an official English translation shall be made in due course. (COP, C, 13.4)*

In the case of someone who is 'deaf' or 'speech handicapped', 'the interviewing officer shall ensure that the interpreter is given an opportunity to read the record of the interview and to certify its accuracy in the event of his being called to give evidence.' (COP, C, 13.7).

WHEN SHOULD AN APPROPRIATE ADULT OR INTERPRETER BE CALLED?

The new 1995 Code sets out certain groups of people for whom the appropriate adult does not apply, which do not affect the appropriate adult role (COP, C, 1.12).

The duty to call an appropriate adult is clearly set out in the Code and can only be delayed if circumstances pertain as set out in Annex C of Code C.

(1) *If the (detained) person is a juvenile, is mentally handicapped, or appears to be suffering from mental disorder, then the custody officer must as soon as practicable inform the appropriate adult (who in the case of a juvenile may or may not be a person responsible for her/his welfare in accordance with paragraph 3.7 of Code C of the grounds for his detention, and his whereabouts, and ask the adult to come to the police station to see the person (COP, C, 3.9)*

unless Annex C applies, which states that:

If, and only if, an officer of the rank of Superintendent or above considers that delay will lead to the consequences set out in paragraph 11.1(a) to (c) of this Code:

> (a) *a person heavily under the influence of drink or drugs may be interviewed in that state; or*
>
> (b) *an arrested juvenile or a person who is mentally disordered or mentally handicapped may be interviewed in the absence of the appropriate adult; or*
>
> (c) *a person who has difficulty in understanding English or who has a hearing disability may be interviewed in the absence of an interpreter' (Annex C, COP,C, Page 72, paragraph 1).*

Although

> (2) *Questioning in these circumstances may not continue once sufficient information to avert the immediate risk has been obtained,' and 'a record shall be made of the grounds for any decision to interview a person under paragraph one above', (Annex C, COP, C, page 72, paragraphs 2 and 3). In addition, although it is only a Note of Guidance (CI), to these provisions, Annex C also states that:*
>
> *The special groups referred to in this Annex are all particularly vulnerable. The provisions of the annex, which override safeguards designed to protect them and to minimise the risk of interviews producing unreliable evidence, should be applied only in exceptional cases of need.*

Appropriate adults will want to take particular note if they discover on arrival at the police station that this Note of Guidance has not been adhered to, since, although its legal status is tenuous, it may be important in subsequent negotiations with the police, either at the time or in a social worker's agency making representation to the police at a management level, and for the detainee's solicitor to know of this in her/his work for the detainee.

A new section 1.1A in the 1995 Codes state that a custody officer is required to perform the functions specified in the role as soon as is practicable, but will not be in breach of the Code in the event of delay, provided that it is justifiable, and that every reasonable step is taken to prevent this; reasons will be recorded in the custody record. There might be a large number of suspects at the same time, no interview rooms being available, or there are difficulties in contacting an appropriate adult, solicitor or interpreter (NOG, 1H).

WHO IS AN APPROPRIATE ADULT?

The definition varies slightly for the different vulnerable groups.

While it was possible under the 1985 Codes of Practice for a solicitor acting in a professional capacity to be the appropriate adult, this was no longer possible in the 1991 Codes, nor is it possible under the 1995 Codes. 'A solicitor or lay visitor who is present at the station in that capacity may not act as the appropriate adult.' (COP, C, NOG, 1F).

Juveniles

In order of preference:

* the parent, guardian, or, if he is in care, his care authority or voluntary organisation. The new 1995 Codes define 'in care' to cover all cases in which a juvenile is 'looked after' by a local authority under the terms of the Children Act 1989;

* a social worker (who could be in residential, daycare, or field work employed by social services departments, probation, or a voluntary agency);

* failing either of the above categories, another responsible adult aged 18 or over, who is not a police officer, or employed by the police (COP, C, 1.7(a)).

Where the juvenile is known to be subject to a supervision order, reasonable steps must also be taken to notify the supervising officer (COP, C, 3.8).

An exception to the above order of preference comes into play if the following applies:

> *A person including a parent or guardian of a juvenile should not be the appropriate adult if he is suspected of involvement in the offence in question, is the victim, is a witness, is involved in the investigation or has received admissions prior to attending as an appropriate adult. If the parent of a juvenile is estranged from the juvenile, he should not be*

asked to act as the appropriate adult if the juvenile expressly and specifically objects to his presence. (COP, C, NOG, 1C)

If a juvenile admits an offence to or in the presence of a social worker other than during the time that the social worker is acting as an appropriate adult for that juvenile, another social worker should be the appropriate adult in the interest of fairness. (COP, NOG, 1B)

Juveniles should not be interviewed at their places of education except in exceptional circumstances, and then only where the principal or his nominee agrees, and only where there would be 'unreasonable delay' by awaiting his/her presence should an interview take place without the appropriate adult's presence. In these circumstances, 'the principal or his nominee can act as the appropriate adult', except where the suspected offence is against the educational establishment itself (COP,C,11.15).

If the juvenile 'is in the care' of a local authority or voluntary organisation, but is living with parents or other adults responsible for his or her welfare, the police should try to inform them as well as the care authority, unless they are believed to be involved in the offence concerned; they should also try to inform parents even if the juvenile is not living with them. There is, however, no legal duty for the police to carry out these actions (COP, C, NOG 3C).

In the case of a person who is mentally disordered or who is mentally handicapped

In order of preference:

- a relative, guardian, or other person responsible for his or her care or custody;

- someone who has experience of dealing with mentally disordered or mentally handicapped persons, but is not a police officer or employed by the police (such as an approved social worker as defined by the Mental Health Act 1983 or a specialist social worker); or

- failing either of the above, some other responsible adult aged 18 or over who is not a police officer or employed by the police (COP, C, 1.7(b)).

The Note of Guidance 1E in Code C states that: 'In the case of persons who are mentally disordered or mentally handicapped, it may in certain circumstances be more satisfactory for all concerned if the appropriate adult is someone who has experience or training in their care rather than a relative lacking such qualifications. But if the person himself prefers a relative to a better qualified stranger his wishes should if practicable be respected.' If a social worker is called under this provision s/he should check that the detainee understands the options, and his/her choice is followed through. There is no reason why a carer plus a social worker or other professional acting as an appropriate adult should not attend together to fulfil the different roles needed here.

The same reasons as for juveniles apply for excluding someone from acting as an appropriate adult for these groups (COP,C, NOG, IC).

Workers and other professionals in day care, residential settings, or fieldwork for these user groups should make themselves aware of this guidance, and the need to have ready access to guidelines on what the role of the appropriate adult entails. Other professionals who might be called, (for example community nurses) may also need to avail themselves of such information, as well as others involved in voluntary groups who might be called, e.g. MENCAP or MIND.

Special note concerning people detained under section 135 or section 136 of the Mental Health Act 1983

The 1991 Codes for the first time included reference to this group of people, who are detained under mental health legislation, and not under criminal legislation. They did not, however, include the safeguards concerning reviews of detention in section 15 of Code C (COP, C, 1.10). There may be arguments that these provisions should cover those detained under mental health legislation. This is maintained in the 1995 Codes.

It is imperative that a mentally disordered or mentally handicapped person who has been detained under Section 136 of the Mental Health Act 1983 should be assessed as soon as possible. If that assessment is to take place at the police station, an approved social worker and a registered medical practitioner should be called to the police station as soon as possible to interview and examine the person. Once the person has been interviewed and examined and suitable arrangements have been made for his treatment or care, he can no longer be detained under Section 136. The person should not be released until he has been seen by both the approved social worker and the registered medical practitioner. (COP, C, 3.10)

Those who are blind, seriously visually handicapped, and those unable to read

For those covered by this section, 'The custody officer should ensure that his solicitor, relative, the appropriate adult, or some other person likely to take an interest in him, (and not involved in the investigation) is available to help in checking any documentation'. This person may also sign on behalf of the detainee if the latter agrees (COP, C, 3.14 and NOG 3F).

Those unable to communicate in English, who appear to be deaf, or where there is doubt about hearing or speaking ability

The police are not required to call an appropriate adult, but 'the custody officer must, as soon as practicable, call an interpreter', if the officer is unable to establish effective communication with the detainee, and ask the interpreter to provide the required information to the detainee about his/her rights (see page 47) (COP, C, 3.6).

A person whose speaking or hearing ability is in doubt 'must not be interviewed in the absence of an interpreter unless he agrees in writing to be interviewed without one, or if paragraph 11.1 or Annex C (of the Codes of Practice, section C) applies.' (COP,C, 13.5).

Where a detained juvenile's parent(s) or guardian(s) are hearing or speech disabled, the interview should not proceed without an interpreter unless paragraph 11.1 or Annex C (of Codes of Practice section C) applies, or s/he agrees in writing (COP, C, 13.6).

The police are referred to social services departments for information on interpreters for those with a hearing disability, and to Community Relations Councils for those who do not understand English (COP, C, NOG, 3D). In addition, an interpreter 'may make a telephone call or write a letter on a person's behalf.' (COP, C, NOG 5A).

CAUTIONARY NOTE FOR NON-RELATIVES CALLED ON TO ACT AS AN APPROPRIATE ADULT

Ensure that all efforts have been made to contact the parent(s) or guardian(s). The duty of the police to do this quickly is set out on page 34. If necessary, make it clear that you will also try to secure their attendance. Attempts should be made to contact them by telephone, via relatives or friends, or by calling at their home to discuss the situation. If it becomes clear that the police did not perform their duties properly, this should be reported to the custody officer, and the parent or guardian, as the latter may wish to take this matter up with the police, or the solicitor. The non-relative should also inform the appropriate manager in their agency where appropriate. In some circumstances parents or guardians are precluded from attending as the appropriate adult. (See 'Who is an Appropriate Adult?', page 36.)

This further contact is especially important where the parent or guardian is refusing to attend; there is a clear role here for conciliation and mediation work. Further attempts to make contact increase the chances of securing the attendance of someone who knows the young person. The Codes indicate that a social worker or other non-relative is preferable to another 'responsible adult' who is known to the detainee, but this could be negotiable if the circumstances indicated that this latter option would be better for the detainee.

If the social worker or other non-relative does negotiate the attendance of a parent, guardian or other person, s/he should ensure that this person knows the main elements of the role, and knows the rights of the detainee, as there is no duty for the police or a solicitor to do this, and appropriate adults are not given any specific guidance on their duties. The only requirement on the police is to inform him/her that s/he is there not merely as an observer, but also to advise the person being questioned; to observe the interview is being conducted fairly and properly; and to facilitate communication with the interviewee. There is no duty to tell him/her how best they can carry out these tasks, and be able to act appropriately. The British Association of Social Workers has been in communication with the Home Office to attempt to change this situation.

In addition, social workers need to be very careful in explaining what their role is to the detainee, in particular in relation to admissions of guilt; the repercussions of their actions in this area are potentially great (see pages 55-57).

4 AT THE POLICE STATION

THE APPROPRIATE ADULT AT THE POLICE STATION AND THEIR ROLE IN CALLING FOR LEGAL ADVICE

Check that relatives or other more suitable appropriate adults, who know the young person well, are still unavailable, as even a short period of time may render them available, or more amenable to attend the police station after discussion with a social worker or other non-relative about the desirability of their doing so.

On arrival, check that there is at least one poster in the charging area of the station, advertising the right to have free legal advice, and that this poster contains translations into Welsh, the main ethnic minority languages, and the principal EC languages wherever these are likely to be helpful, and it is practicable to do so (COP, C, 6.3 and NOG 6H).

Before any questions are asked by the police, check:

- that no 'informal statements' have been given or taken in the absence of a solicitor or appropriate adult which might prejudice the interview. The ground needs to be fully cleared of any prior 'understandings' that the police or detainee have of what has already taken place, and how that might impact on the pending interview.

- The appropriate adult should intervene if it seems that reference is being made to any such 'understandings' worked up between the interviewing officer(s) and the detainee, to ensure that no misconceptions are left over from any previous 'informal' discussions, and how these relate to the formal interview.

- how long the person has been detained under arrest at the police station, and make a note of it. This may be important later in reviews of the period of detention.

- that the detainee has been informed of the exact grounds for detention before any questioning takes place (COP, C, 3.4). If a detainee is not arrested, s/he is free to leave at any time (PACE, s.29), unless s/he is placed under arrest. Even if the detainee is attending the station on a voluntary basis, s/he has a right to consult a solicitor free of charge at any time during a detention.

- The names of the interviewing and custody officers (not available in Prevention of Terrorism legislation interviews).

The detainee has a right to communicate privately, in person, in writing, or on the telephone with the solicitor (COP, C, 6.1), and a new NOG, 1EE in the 1995 Codes states that this is true even where the detainee does not want the appropriate adult present for this.

It is vital that the appropriate adult is aware of the possibility of their calling a solicitor on the client's behalf at all times. The police may not have stated clearly to the detainee that s/he would not have to pay for the solicitor up to a certain time limit, as this is paid for by the Legal Aid Scheme. The detainee's own solicitor can be contacted, or the Duty Solicitor Scheme where this is in operation, and if s/he does not wish or is unable to use these means, s/he should be given an opportunity to choose a solicitor from a list of those willing to provide legal advice, with up to two alternatives if the first is not available; the custody officer can allow further attempts at her/his discretion (COP, C, NOG 6B). A new NOG, 1I states that it is important for the custody officer to remind the appropriate adult and detainee of this right and reasons for waiving it under section 6 of Code C.

This right can only be delayed if Annex B of Code C applies (see page 46). (COP, C, 6.5).

The appropriate adult has the right to call a solicitor on behalf of the detainee (COP, C, 3.13); the purpose of this is to protect the rights of the detainee, 'who may not understand the significance of what is being said to him. If such a person wishes to exercise the right to legal advice, the appropriate action should be taken straight away and not delayed until the appropriate adult arrives.' (COP, C, NOG 3G).

As the appropriate adult, with your knowledge of the Act and Codes, if you believe that there is an infringement of them, or that the detainee needs legal advice over their questioning or statement, you should advise the detainee of their right to consult a solicitor at any stage, and that they have a right to say or sign nothing until they have done so. If the appropriate adult believes a solicitor is necessary, and the detainee does not appreciate the importance of calling one, the appropriate adult should do this on her/his behalf. In addition, the police should not try to dissuade the suspect from obtaining legal advice (COP, C, 6.4).

However the police may require an interview to continue if:

- the person consents in writing or on tape to the interview going ahead (it is not clear from the Codes whether this is the detainee him/herself, the parent, guardian, or other appropriate adult, where the detainee falls into one of the vulnerable groups); or

- the police superintendent believes that delay in awaiting a solicitor will involve an immediate risk of harm to persons or serious loss of, or damage to property (COP, C, 6.6 (b)(i)); or

- a solicitor, including a duty solicitor, has been contacted and has agreed to attend, but awaiting his or her arrival would cause undesirable delay to the process of investigation (COP, C, 6.6(b)(ii)); or

- the person's own solicitor or a solicitor selected from a list is unavailable, or in this case or previously has declined to attend, or cannot be contacted. If this is the case, the detainee must be advised of the Duty Solicitor Scheme. The interview may continue if the detainee has declined to ask for the duty solicitor, or the duty solicitor is not available. The interview can only be started or continued provided an officer of at least the rank of inspector agrees to this (COP, C, 6.6 (c) and NOG 6B); or

- where Annex B of Code C applies. This was a much contested inclusion in the Codes. It means that the detainee may be held without access to a solicitor, where 'the person is in police detention in connection with a serious arrestable offence, and has not yet been charged.' An appropriate adult may then be present when a solicitor is barred, making it vital s/he knows how to carry out their role effectively.

The 1995 Code allows an interview to continue if the detainee, having previously asked for legal advice, then declines it, and an inspector or above agrees. Confirmation of the detainee's agreement, or change of mind, to go ahead without legal advice must be recorded (COP, C6.6(d)).

The rights referred to may also be delayed where the serious arrestable offence is either:

• a drug trafficking offence and the officer has reasonable grounds for believing that the detained person has benefited from drug trafficking, and that the recovery of the value of that person's proceeds from this will be hindered by the exercise of either right; or

• an offence to which Part VI of the Criminal Justice Act 1988 (covering confiscation orders) applies, in which case the same criteria apply as the first item (COP, C, Annex B, 2).

Notes B4 and B5 state that in the case of paragraph 1 of Annex B, Code C, the 'officer may authorise delaying access to a specific solicitor only if he has reasonable grounds to believe that specific solicitor will, inadvertently or otherwise, pass on a message from the detained person or act in some other way which will lead to any of the three results in paragraph 1 coming about. In these circumstances the officer should offer the detained person access to a solicitor (who is not the specific solicitor referred to above) on the Duty Solicitor Scheme.' (COP, C, Annex B, NOG B4). The fact that the grounds for delaying notification of arrest under paragraph 1 may be satisfied does not automatically mean that the grounds for delaying access to legal advice will also be satisfied. (COP, C, Annex B, NOG B5) Whilst these parts of the codes have changed from the 1985 codes, making police go through procedures of informing the Law Society, for example, to ensure such actions are challenged, such exclusion is still possible. The police can bar a non-accredited or probationary representative from advising the detainee, though all should now be accredited for such work (COPC, 6.12 to 6.14).

The police must also give reminders of the right to free legal advice, in accordance with paragraphs 3.5, 16.4 and 16.5 of Code C, and 2.15(ii) of Code D, (concerning group identification or video identification), and 5.2 of Code D (concerning intimate body samples), at the commencement and re-commencement of an interview (COP, C, 11.2), and at the time of a review (COP, C, 15.3). The interviewing officer must enter into the custody record that these reminders have been given.

Differentiation between the role of the solicitor and the appropriate adult

The 1991 and 1995 Codes make it clear that a solicitor (or lay visitor) acting in that capacity cannot also act as an appropriate adult under the Act and Codes of Practice (COP, C, NOG 1F). The solicitor is there solely to protect her/his client's interests; the appropriate adult has a broader role than this (see page 5).

It is also important, because of this differentiation in role, that the appropriate adult meets with the detainee on their own initially without the solicitor. This is because of the problem of an appropriate adult receiving 'admissions' of guilt. In a recent case reported by the Law Society a social worker employed by a local authority had been directed by their employer to disclose admissions they have received from detainees to the police. It is recommended that appropriate adults see the detainee on their own to explain the limits and boundaries of their role, and to advise that they are not there to receive admissions, and to convey the possible consequences of such admissions. Appropriate adults have a right to see detainees on their own before anything else occurs (COP, C, 3.12). For fuller discussion of these points, see page 54.

Ensure that the detainee has been informed of their rights by the custody officer both verbally and in writing.

The custody officer must inform the detainee that s/he need not exercise their rights immediately.

Right 1

The right to have someone informed of his or her arrest, in accordance with section 5 of COP, C, and COP, C, 3.1(i).

Right 2

The right to consult privately with a solicitor at any time in accordance with section 6 of COP, C, in private, any such independent legal advice being free of charge. This may be in person, in writing or by telephone (COP, C, 3.1(ii), 6.1 and 6.5, NOG 6B and 6J). A police officer should not advise on any particular firm of solicitors, and the detainee must be informed of the arrival of the solicitor unless Annex B applies (COP, C, 6.15). If the detainee refuses legal advice, the officer will point out that s/he may consult a solicitor over the telephone. If s/he still refuses, s/he will be asked why, and any reply recorded in the custody or interview record (COP, C, 6.5).

Right 3

The right to consult the Codes of Practice (COP, C, 3.1(iii)) though NOG 3E says this right does not entitle the detainee to delay unreasonably any necessary investigative or administrative action while s/he does so, in particular the provision of breath, blood, or urine specimens under the Road Traffic Act 1988.

The notices of entitlements to rights should be available in Welsh, the main ethnic minority and principal European languages where this is likely to be helpful (COP, NOG 3B, and NOG 6H). If a detainee is 'incapable at the time of understanding what is said to him or is violent or likely to become violent or is in urgent need of medical attention, he must be given it as soon as practicable.' This is in relation to the notice of rights, or any other information the detainee has to be given under the codes.

The custody officer should not invite comment from the detainee on the arresting officer's account, or on a decision to detain him/her (COP, C, 3.4).

In addition, the detainee has a right to silence (see paragraph on cautioning on page 49), but the detainee must have it made clear to him/her that exercising this right may lead to inference of guilt in a subsequent court case.

If a detainee is a citizen of an independent Commonwealth country or a national of a foreign country (including the Republic of Ireland), s/he must be informed as soon as practicable of her/his rights of communication with his/her High Commission, Embassy, or Consulate (COP, C, 3.3). See section 7 of Code C for a full exposition of such detainees' rights.

It is interesting to note that there is a right to see the Codes, but no legal right to see the Act.

In addition to the three rights detailed above, the custody officer must give in the written notice setting out these rights, the information that s/he has a right to the custody record copy which will be made, and the caution which was administered to her/him. The custody officer will ask the person to sign the custody record and acknowledge receipt of this notice and to confirm his/her decision on whether s/he wishes to have legal advice at this point (COP, C, 3.2 and 3.5). This must be done in the presence of the appropriate adult, whether done previously in his/her absence or not (COP, C, 3.11). The detainee does not have to give reasons for declining legal advice (COP, C, NOG, 6K). It should also include the arrangements for obtaining legal advice, (a new requirement in the 1991 Codes) and brief notes on the rights of the detainee whilst in custody, e.g. visits, and contacts with outside parties, physical conditions, arrangements for food and drink, toileting, clothing, exercise, and medical attention (COP, C, NOG 3A).

The person acting as an appropriate adult should ensure that the detainee is fully aware of their rights, has had the written notice and has signed the custody record to acknowledge receipt of the notice.

Where the detained person is a juvenile, is mentally handicapped, or is suffering from mental disorder the custody officer must inform the appropriate adult of the grounds for detention, and ask them to attend as soon as possible. If the appropriate adult is already at the police station, then the custody officer must ensure that this information concerning the detainee's rights is given in the appropriate adult's presence in order to ensure that they are fully understood and acted upon where necessary, and that 'if the appropriate adult is not at the police station when the information is given then the information must be given to the detained person again in the presence of the appropriate adult.' (COP, C, 3.11). The detainee should be advised by the custody officer that the 'appropriate adult (where applicable) is there to assist and advise him and that he can consult privately with the appropriate adult at any time.' (COP, C, 3.12).

CAUTIONING

The appropriate adult must ensure that any detainee who is a juvenile, who is mentally handicapped, or mentally disordered is cautioned properly before questioning commences, in the following manner, when the officer has grounds to suspect a person of an offence (COP, C, 10.1). If this has happened prior to the appropriate adult's arrival, it must be repeated in the appropriate adult's presence (COP, C, 10.6). This is a new requirement in the 1991 Codes, and the appropriate adult should ensure the detainee understands the consequences of it.

There are some major changes which result from a general review of procedures and the enactment of the Criminal Justice and Public Order Act 1994, sections 36 and 37, relating to the fundamental change in English law brought about by the Act. As a result of this change a court can draw inference of guilt if a suspect chooses to exercise her/his right to silence.

The new caution

The full text of Code C in relation to cautions is reproduced below, as it is a more important element now than it was before the 1994 Criminal Justice and Public Order Act.

10 Cautions

(a) When a caution must be given

10.1 *A person whom there are grounds to suspect of an offence must be cautioned before any questions about it (or further questions if it is his answers to previous questions which provide the grounds for suspicion) are put to him regarding his involvement or suspected involvement in that offence if his answers or his silence (i.e. failure or refusal to answer a question or to answer satisfactorily) may be given in evidence to a court in a prosecution. He therefore need not be cautioned if questions are put for other purposes, for example, solely to establish his identity or his ownership of any vehicle or to obtain information in accordance with any relevant statutory requirement (see paragraph 10.5C) or in furthermore of the proper and effective conduct of a search, (for example to determine the need to search in the exercise of powers of stop and search or to seek co-operation while carrying out a search) or to seek verification of a written record in accordance with paragraph 11.13.*

10.2 *Whenever a person who is not under arrest is initially cautioned or is reminded that he is under caution (see paragraph 10.5) he must at the same time be told that he is not under arrest and is not obliged to remain with the officer (see paragraph 3.15).*

10.3 *A person must be cautioned upon arrest for an offence unless:*

(a)it is impracticable to do so by reason of his condition or behaviour at the time; or

(b)he has already been cautioned immediately prior to arrest in accordance with paragraph 10.1 above.

(b) Action: general

10.4 *The caution shall be in the following terms:*

You do not have to say anything. But it may harm your defence if you do not mention when questioned something which you later rely on in court. Anything you do say may be given in evidence.

Minor deviations do not constitute a breach of the requirement provided that the sense of the caution is preserved. [See Note 10C]

10.5 *When there is a break in questioning under caution the interviewing officer must ensure that the person being questioned is aware that he remains under caution. If there is any doubt the caution shall be given again in full when the interview resumes. [See Note 10A].*

Special warnings under section 36 and 37 of the Criminal Justice Public Order Act 1994

10.5A *When a suspect who is interviewed after arrest fails or refuses to answer certain questions, or to answer them satisfactorily, after due warning, a court or jury may draw such inferences as appear proper under sections 36 and 37 of the Criminal Justice and Public Order Act 1994. This applies when:*

(a) a suspect is arrested by a constable and there is found on his person, or in or on his clothing or footwear, or otherwise in his possession, or in the place where he was arrested, any objects, marks or substances, or marks on such objects, and the person fails or refuses to account for the objects, marks or substances found; or

(b) an arrested person was found by a constable at a place at or about the time the offence for which he was arrested, is alleged to have been committed, and the person fails or refuses to account for his presence at that place.

10.5B *For an inference to be drawn from a suspect's failure or refusal to answer a question about one of these matters or to answer it satisfactorily, the interviewing officer must first tell him in ordinary language:*

(a) what offence he is investigating;

(b) what fact he is asking the suspect to account for;

(c) that he believes this fact may be due to the suspect's taking part in the commission of the offence in question;

(d) that a court may draw a proper inference if he fails or refuses to account for the fact about which he is being questioned;

(e) that a record is being made of the interview and that it may be given in evidence if he is brought to trial.

10.5C *Where, despite the fact that a person has been cautioned, failure to co-operate may have an effect on his immediate treatment, he should be informed of any relevant consequences and that they are not affected by the caution. Examples are when his refusal to provide his name and address when charged may render him liable to detention, or when his refusal to provide particulars and information in accordance with a statutory requirement, for example, under the Road Traffic Act 1988, may amount to an offence or may make him liable to arrest.*

(c) Juveniles, the mentally disordered and the mentally handicapped

10.6 *If a juvenile or a person who is mentally disordered or mentally handicapped is cautioned in the absence of the appropriate adult, the caution must be repeated in the adult's presence.*

(d) Documentation

10.7 *A record shall be made when a caution is given under this section, either in the officer's pocket book or in the interview record as appropriate.*

Notes for Guidance

10A *In considering whether or not to caution again after a break, the officer should bear in mind that he may have to satisfy a court that the person understood that he was still under caution when the interview resumed.*

10B *[Not used]*

10C *If it appears that a person does not understand what the caution means, the officer who has given it should go on to explain it in his own words.*

The appropriate adult will want to ensure that the caution takes place, and that the detainee understands the effects of what is being said to him/her. It is at this point that legal advice should be considered again and it should also be ensured that the detainee understands fully their rights at the beginning of the questioning procedure.

The courts have to know that the appropriate adult has properly performed their functions and duties with regard to the detainee to ensure that justice was done.

If the person was not under arrest but is told, whether at a police station or not, that s/he is being placed under caution, either before or during an interview, the person must be told s/he is not under arrest, and is not obliged to remain with the officer. The detainee must be told of her/his right to free legal advice if s/he wishes (COP, C, 3.15 and 10.2).

THE ROLE OF THE APPROPRIATE ADULT IN THE INTERVIEW

The Codes of Practice quoted on page 5 of these guidelines clearly define the role of appropriate adult (COP, C, 11.16), and an important new statement was inserted in NOG, 11B, Code C and retained in the 1995 Codes: 'It is important to bear in mind that, although juveniles or persons who are mentally disordered or mentally handicapped are often capable of providing reliable evidence, they may, without knowing or wishing to do so, be particularly prone in certain circumstances to provide information which is unreliable, misleading or self-incriminating. Special care should therefore always be exercised in questioning such a person, and the appropriate adult should be involved, if there is any doubt about a person's age, mental state or capacity. Because of the risk of unreliable evidence it is also important to obtain corroboration of any facts admitted whenever possible.' (COP, C, NOG 11B).

This statement was made due to certain situations where wrongful actions have been taken by police and courts because of these reasons, most recently in the case of David McKenzie released from Rampton in 1992. The role of the appropriate adult is vital in such situations.

Explaining your role to the detainee

The appropriate adult has a right to see the detained person in private, at any time, and should always do so on arrival at the police station before any formal interviewing takes place (see page 55) to explain their role and function (COP, C, 3.12). The custody officer should also have explained the appropriate adult's role to the detainee, that is, to advise and assist him/her, and that the detainee has the right to see the appropriate adult in private at any time (COP, C, 3.12). The vital importance of this to the appropriate adult is set out on page 47 and below.

Conflict of roles of appropriate adult and solicitor

As we have seen, a solicitor acting in his/her professional capacity cannot act as an appropriate adult. You are strongly advised to see the detainee alone before the interview begins, and without the solicitor if one is already present. This is important in order to ensure that the detainee recognises the difference in role between the appropriate adult and the solicitor; and, more crucially, that the detainee is made aware of what an admission of guilt may mean, i.e. that the appropriate adult cannot guarantee that this information will not be passed on to the police. The solicitor can, of course guarantee this confidentiality. There are several reasons for this.

• Social workers may face a particular problem. The British Association of Social Workers' Code of Ethics states that the social worker 'recognises that information clearly entrusted for one purpose should not be used for another purpose without sanction. S/he respects the privacy of clients and confidential information about clients gained in his/her relationship with them or others. S/he will divulge such information only with the consent of the informant except where there is clear evidence of serious danger to the client, worker, other person or the community, in other circumstances judged exceptional, on the basis of professional consideration and consultation.' This means that on occasions, if these conditions apply, confidentiality may have to be breached. Before doing so, social workers should confer with the managers in their agencies, and their professional association if it is a serious matter.

• For others as well as for social workers, further complications arise from Note of Guidance 1B in Code C which states that 'when a police officer is trying to discover whether, or by whom, an offence has been committed, he is entitled to question any person from whom he thinks useful information can be obtained, subject to the restrictions imposed by this code. A person's declaration that he is unwilling to reply does not alter this statement.' The first part of this note states that 'This code does not affect the principle that all citizens have a duty to help police officers to prevent crime and discover offenders. This is a civic rather than a legal duty.' The implcation of this is that if an appropriate adult withdraws as a result of having received an admission, the police may pursue this with the detainee and/or the appropriate adult. In these circumstances, the detainee should be reminded of her/his rights if the appropriate adult decides to withdraw: the right to free legal advice obtained before the formal interview begins; the right to remain silent; and the requirement that an appropriate adult is present. The appropriate adult may wish to arrange to speak with the next appropriate adult, but will obviously need to be guarded in what s/he says concerning any admission.

• In 1992, a social worker consulted on the issue of an admission they had received. The Director of Social Services instructed the social worker to inform the police of this admission. Others acting for agencies, as workers or volunteers, may find themselves in similar situations.

• The Police and Criminal Evidence Act allows the police, in certain circumstances, to search employing agencies files (see chapter 7). It is therefore important that workers consider very carefully what is put on a client's file, including any admission of 'guilt' a client may have made.

For these three reasons, social workers and others acting as appropriate adults are strongly advised to set out these points to the detainee before any other discussions take place, and in private, without a solicitor or other person present. This is because an 'admission' may well be made in the presence of the solicitor, but will have a different status from what the appropriate adult may have to do with such information. S/he is also advised to say that s/he may have to leave if given an admission of guilt, that this may subsequently have to be passed on to the police, and another appropriate adult will have to be found. The detainee will need to be told the police may then surmise that an admission was made. Initially, however, before consultation, the social worker is advised to say they cannot impart the reason for their withdrawal, and that there may indeed be several reasons why such a professional decision needs to be made. The Law Society is also advising that the first consultations with the detainee should be separate for the solicitor and the appropriate adult, with further consultations being determined by taking account of any risk of disclosure and the wishes of the detainee. This means it is important for the solicitor and appropriate adult to ensure they consult about this before further private consultations with the detainee.

It should be noted that there is no provision legally, or in the Codes, to require the appropriate adult to withdraw in such circumstances, except where 'if a juvenile in care admits an offence to or in the presence of a social worker other than during the time that the social worker is acting as the appropriate adult for that juvenile, another social worker should be the appropriate adult in the interest of fairness.' (COP, C, NOG, 1D). This is new in the 1995 Codes. Previously, the Codes stated that the social worker should withdraw if a child in care admits an offence.

In the 1995 Codes, the detainee can now ask to see his/her solicitor without the appropriate adult (COP, C, NOG, 1EE).

EXPLAINING THE TERMS OF THE INTERVIEW

There is a clear duty for the appropriate adult to ensure that the detainee understands what is being asked of her/him, and the implications of certain ways of answering. The appropriate adult should, if necessary, interrupt the interview to satisfy her/himself that the detainee understands what is being asked, and the meaning of her/his reply, to ensure s/he really means to say it in that way. Certain methods of questioning, such as 'leading' questions, can confuse or intimidate the detainee, and may need the intervention of the appropriate adult to help him/her think clearly about the response. The detainee should be encouraged to use their own statements about events and incidents, and should not allow themselves to be led into a 'yes' or 'no' answer, other than over simple factual matters, e.g. their name, address, etc. The appropriate adult will ideally keep contemporaneous notes of the interview. Not only could these be of value later but, it also shows to all concerned that s/he is taking her/his role seriously.

An appropriate adult or interpreter could be called to a subsequent court hearing if aspects of a detention, and/or interview s/he has attended are questioned by the defence solicitor, so it is important the role be carried out effectively and in accordance with the Codes.

The Codes state that 'no police officer may try to obtain answers to questions or elicit a statement by use of oppression. Except as provided for paragraph in 10.5C, no police officer shall indicate, except in answer to a direct question, what action will be taken on the part of the police if the person being interviewed answers questions, makes a statement or refuses to do either.' (COP, C, 11.3). Make a record of any offensive or racist remarks; if any have been made inform parents/guardians and the detainee's solicitor, if there is one. Take up the issue through your employing agency where appropriate or directly with police management.

Check once again that the detainee clearly understands your role; often the speed of events and wish to get out of the police station can lead to confusion and an attitude of resignation, and s/he may need to be reminded of the responsibility and effects of your role. Often the detainee feels s/he has no rights, or does not know how to assert them. Appropriate adults have a duty to help compensate for these feelings of powerlessness that the client experiences. The overwhelming temptation especially for the vulnerable groups can often be to get it all over and done with, and sometimes the easiest way at that moment is to admit the offence.

If a break in questioning occurs, ensure that the detainee is aware of exactly when the interview formally starts again to avoid any confusion over this. The interviewing officer must also state again that the detainee has a right to free legal advice if s/he has not availed her/himself of this already.

The appropriate adult should be aware of several attendant rights of the detainee. These are:

• The general right not to be held incommunicado.

• To have three attempts to contact someone 'who is likely to take an interest in his welfare, at public expense, as soon as possible of his whereabouts,' and that the person in charge of the detention or the investigation has discretion to allow further attempts until the information has been conveyed (COP, C, 5.1), and that this may only be delayed in accordance with Annex B of Code C (see page 46), and COP, C, NOG, 5D.

• Unless the detention is in pursuance of the Prevention of Terrorism (Temporary Provisions) Act 1989, or Annex B of Code C applies, the detainee should on request be provided with writing materials to send a note, and be allowed to speak to or telephone for a reasonable length of time one person (COP, C, 5.6). These provisions are unlikely to be important to the vulnerable groups discussed here, as their right to an appropriate adult is separate from and in addition to these rights (COP, C, 3.7). The detainee should be told the letter may be read, and the telephone call listened in to, and used in evidence. In addition, interpreters may write or telephone on the detainee's behalf (COP, C, NOG, 5A).

Check what the detainee has been asked prior to your arrival, and whether this was under caution or not. Explain to her/him that any questions asked prior to your arrival do not have relevance now — a new set of questions, with the codes and with your role involved, will now be put and it is not just a continuation of any conversations s/he and the police had before. This is important, so that the detainee does not have a distorted understanding of events and procedures, leading to her/him answering in 'shorthand', without full details. If this does occur, it may lead to a distorted view of the detainee's involvement in any alleged offence, and influence the Crown Prosecution Service in decisions to prosecute or not, and any court which will have subsequent sight of it. In any event, the detainee should not have been formally questioned in transit between different police forces, except in order to clarify any voluntary statement made by him/her, nor in a hospital without the agreement of a responsible doctor (COP, C, 14.1 and 14.2).

A DUTY TO ENSURE THE LEGAL RIGHTS OF THE DETAINEE

In addition to the duties as set out above, there is also a general duty on the appropriate adult to 'make representations', at the review officer's discretion, at times of reviews (see page 69). (COP, C, 15.1).

The role of the appropriate adult also lays responsibility on the person fulfilling this role to ensure that the conditions of detention are followed as outlined below, and that a solicitor is contacted when this would seem to be in the detainee's interests (see page 70).

The rights of the detainee under her/his conditions of detention are:

1   The right to medical help whenever this seems necessary. (See COP, C, 9.2 to 9.9, and NOG, 9A, 9B and 9C, concerning the police's specific duties in this area). Police officers may not administer medicines which are also controlled drugs under the Misuse of Drugs Act 1971.
2   Cells should be adequately heated, cleaned, ventilated, lit; lights should be able to be dimmed. They should allow sleep, safety, and security (COP, C, 8.2).

3 No additional restraints should be used within a locked cell unless absolutely necessary, and then only suitable handcuffs (COP, C, 8.2).

4 To sit down (COP, C, 12.5).

5 To know who the interviewing officer is, and any other officers present, by name and rank, except in the case of detainees under the Prevention of Terrorism (Temporary Provisions) Act 1989, when officers should identify themselves by warrant number and rank only (COP, C, 12.6).

6 Eight hours rest during any twenty-four hour period of detention, free from questioning, travel or interruption arising out of the investigation, normally at night, except where this would:

• involve a risk of harm to persons or serious loss of, or damage to property;

• delay unnecessarily the person's release from custody; or

• otherwise prejudice the outcome of the investigation (COP, C, 12.2). An appropriate adult or solicitor may request this rest be delayed or interrupted under the 1995 Code.

7 Breaks from being interviewed at recognised meal times, plus short breaks for refreshments every two hours, except where the three provisions set out in item 6 exist (COP, C, 8.6 and 12.7).

8 A new requirement in the 1991 codes states that the detainee may receive visitors at the custody officer's discretion (COP, C, 5.4), where there is sufficient manpower to supervise a visit, and it does not effect any possible hindrance to the investigation (COP, C, NOG, 5B).

9 For juveniles not to be placed in a cell with a detained adult, and preferably not in a police cell (COP, C, 8.8).

10 In the case of a mentally handicapped or mentally disordered person, particular care must be taken when deciding whether to use handcuffs (COP, C, 8.2).

If a relative, friend, or person with an interest in the detainee's welfare inquires as to his whereabouts, this information shall be given if the detainee agrees, and where Annex B does not apply (see page 46); although a telephone may not be the appropriate means to communicate such information (COP, C, NOG 5D).

Reasonable force may be used if necessary for the following purposes:

(i) To secure compliance with reasonable instructions, including instructions given in pursuance of the provisions of a code of practice; or

(ii) To prevent escape, injury, damage to property, or the destruction of evidence. (COP, C, 8.9)

The points made in this section of the guide about general duties of the appropriate adult are vital. The appropriate adult has a duty to make a complaint if the Act and Codes are not complied with.

Complaints about a detainee's treatment by the detainee, or on her/his behalf, should be recorded in the custody record, and the custody officer must investigate the complaint (COP, C, 12.8).

The appropriate adult has a duty to make a complaint if the Act and Codes are not observed by the police. The custody officer is personally accountable to a court for any breach of the Codes. It is a formally appointed post within the police service, although COP, C, 1.9 states that any officer who is performing the functions of a custody officer is personally liable in the same way. It is therefore very important that any irregularities are brought to her/his attention. If the appropriate adult is unhappy with the response or decision, they should ask for an entry in the custody record to that effect, together with the grounds for their concern. If a solicitor has not already been called you might well have to involve one now.

Keep notes of these events for any solicitor who may subsequently act for the detainee, as they may prove to be important.

The appropriate adult has the right to tell the detainee that s/he has the right not to say any more until a solicitor arrives (but see pages 49–54). The police can only insist that questioning continues if there is an officer of superintendent rank or above who believes delay would mean immediate risk to people or property; if the detainee agrees to questions continuing; if a solicitor has agreed to attend but unreasonable delay would be caused in the investigation by waiting; if the detainee changes her/his mind; if the solicitor(s) contacted are unavailable or refuse to attend; or if Annex B of Code C applies (COP, C, 6.6). For full details, see the section 'The appropriate adult at the police station and their role in calling for legal advice.' (page 43).

The solicitor has the right to see the detainee in private, as does the appropriate adult. A solicitor can be ordered by the police to leave an interview in exceptional circumstances (COP, C, 6.9 to 6.11). It is not clear from the codes if an appropriate adult can be ordered to leave an interview and no grounds are given in the Codes or Act to justify such an action. The only ground might be as for a solicitor: that his/her 'conduct is such that the investigating officer is unable to properly put questions to the suspect' (COP, C, 6.9). The police force investigating the murder of P.C. Blakelock in the disturbances on Broadwater Farm in 1985 excluded the social worker who had been acting as an appropriate adult for the suspected juveniles. This action was later greatly criticised as it seemed that it may have been because the social worker was advising the detainees clearly of their rights, and representing these to the police force. Eventually the juveniles were acquitted in part because of the conditions of their detention and interview. If a social worker acting as an appropriate adult is excluded s/he should immediately take this to a high level of management in their agency for representations to be made if appropriate, or directly to a more senior officer on duty at the time, in writing as well as verbally, as it is such a serious matter.

Furthermore, even though it is only a Note of Guidance, Code C, Annex B, NOG, B1 states that 'Even if Annex B (concerning delaying notifying a solicitor of a detention) applies in the case of a juvenile, or a person who is mentally disordered or mentally handicapped, action to inform the appropriate adult (and the person responsible for a juvenile's welfare, if that is a different person) must nevertheless be taken in accordance with paragraph 3.7 and 3.9 of this Code', implying that appropriate adults are not open to the same criteria of attendance as solicitors; though, of course, the role is defined partly as being to 'facilitate communication with the person being interviewed' (COP, C, 11.16). If it is a lengthy interview, it would seem that the appropriate adult can change, but there should be good communication at the handover.

INTERVIEW AND CUSTODY RECORDS

The police must make an accurate record, verbatim or summary, of each interview with a person suspected of an offence. This should be made during the course of an interview, or as soon as possible afterwards (COP, C, 11.5, 11.7). It must state the place of the interview, time it begins and ends, the time the record was made (if this is different), any breaks in interviews, and the names of all those present (but see page 60 concerning terrorist offences), and be on official police forms, or in accordance with the Code of Practice on tape recording of interviews (see Chapter 5).

The detainee has the right to write down a statement if s/he wishes (COP, C, Annex D), after caution. The detainee, and the appropriate adult, should be asked to sign saying that it is an accurate record of the interview, or to indicate in what respects s/he considers it inaccurate. If the detainee cannot read or refuses to sign, the senior police officer present will read the record out, and the detainee will be asked to make his/her mark or signature, or indicate where s/he believes it inaccurate (COP, C, 11.10). The appropriate adult will also be given an opportunity to read the record, and sign it; if s/he believes it inaccurate, in consultation with the detainee, s/he should indicate where and how on the record, and ask for this action to be entered into the custody record (COP, C, 11.11). If anyone refuses to sign, the police officer must record this (COP, C, 11.12). If the appropriate adult refuses to sign, a solicitor should be involved for the detainee.

Any comments, included unsolicited comments, which are outside the context of the interview, but which might be relevant to the offence, will be recorded and where possible, the detainee will be given the opportunity to sign it as accurate, or indicate where they believe it is not. Any refusal to sign will be recorded (COP, C, 11.13).

Tape recording of interviews is now the commonest form of interview record, and a separate code of practice has been issued (see Chapter 5).

The custody record is of great importance, in that all information pertaining to the detention and interview must be entered onto it, with times of events. This includes any actions required of an officer of a specified rank and details of the officer's name and rank must be included unless the detention is in pursuance of the Prevention of Terrorism (Temporary Provisions) Act 1989, when only the officer's warrant number and duty station need be recorded (COP, C, 2.2). All actions concerning those in the 'special groups' as defined in Chapter 3 of this guide and the involvement of the appropriate adult and/or interpreters, should be recorded (COP, C, 3.18).

The custody record is the personal responsibility of the custody officer. S/he must ensure the accuracy and completeness of the record, times of events, that notification of rights has been given, reviews are held; etc. (COP, C, 2.3).

Availability of the custody record to detainee, solicitor and appropriate adult

A custody record for each detainee will have been kept from the moment s/he arrived under arrest at the police station, or from when s/he was arrested there after having attended voluntarily (COP, C, 2.1). All entries in the custody record must be timed and dated, be these in writing or on a computer. In the latter case the operator's identification must be included (COP, C, 2.6). The appropriate adult should ask to examine the record before leaving the station. These records are vital in showing whether the full rights of the detainee were upheld, and a copy of them is made available as soon as practicable at the request of the detainee, their legal representative, and the appropriate adult. It was a new requirement for the appropriate adult to have a copy of the record in the 1991 Codes. The 1995 Codes states that a solicitor or appropriate adult must be permitted to consult the custody record as soon as practicable after their arrival at the police station (COP, C, 2.4). A request for it may be made up to 12 months after his/her release (COP, C, 2.4). The same people can request to see the original custody record after the detainee has left the station, if they give reasonable notice. This is also a new right – it was only a Note of Guidance in the Codes prior to 1991.

COP, 2.1 of the 1995 Codes states that any video or audio recording made in the custody area is not part of the custody record. If video is used, a sign stating this must be prominently displayed. It will not be switched off if requested by the detainee (COP, C, 3.5A).

CHARGING AND RELEASING OF DETAINED PERSONS

When an officer considers that there is sufficient evidence for a prosecution to succeed and the person has said all s/he wishes to say, the officer should, without delay, bring her/him before the custody officer who shall then be responsible for considering whether or not the detainee should be charged. If the person is charged with more than one offence, these conditions should be satisfied for each (COP,

C, 16.1), and these and subsequent actions should take place in the presence of the appropriate adult (COP, C, 16.1).

New provisions in the 1991 Codes (and reiterated in the 1995 Codes) mean that when a detainee is charged, s/he shall be cautioned as set out on page 49–54 (COP, C, 16.2), and told s/he is to be prosecuted for an offence by way of a written notice which includes the name of the officer (except in terrorist cases), her/his police station, and the reference number for the case. The detainee should also be told in simple terms the precise offence in law with which s/he is charged. The written notice will begin with the caution, and if the person is a member of one of the vulnerable groups, this notice will also be given to the appropriate adult, as will any statement written by the detainee, or anyone else. The officer should not invite comments on such statements except to caution him/her. If the detainee cannot read, the officer may read it to him/her. People who have difficulties in reading are often embarrassed to admit this, so the appropriate adult should check this with the detainee prior to the commencement of the interview. If a person is charged or informed that s/he may be prosecuted for an offence and a police officer wishes to bring to the notice of that person any written statement made by another person or the content of an interview with another person, the officer will hand a true copy of this to the detainee, but will say or do nothing to invite a reply concerning this, except to say s/he does not have to say anything, but anything s/he does say may be used in evidence, and to remind him/her of the right to free legal advice. If the detainee is from one of the vulnerable groups, the copy will also be given to the appropriate adult (COP, C, 16.3 and 16.4).

Once a detainee has been charged or told s/he is to be charged, no further questions may be put except for preventing or minimising harm or loss to some other person, to clear up an ambiguity in a previous answer or statement, if s/he should have a chance to comment on information obtained since s/he was charged concerning the offence, or informed that s/he may be prosecuted. A caution will be given prior to this latter action (COP, C, 16.5). Contemporaneous records shall be made by the interviewing officer and the Codes for tape recording should be followed if the interview is taped (see Chapter 5) (COP, C, 16.7 and 16.8).

Following charge, the detainee is free to leave unless the custody officer authorises further detention on the grounds that:

(1)   The detainee's address is unknown, or is uncertain;

(2)   Detention is necessary to prevent harm to his/herself or
to others, or loss or damage to property;

(3)   The officer believes the detainee will fail to attend
court or answer to bail, or that detention is necessary
to prevent interference with the administration of
justice or the investigation of an offence or offences.
(PACE, s.38(1))

Juveniles may also be detained after charge if the custody officer believes that this would be in the detainee's own interests (PACE, s.38 (1b)). The Act and Codes do not clarify what these might be. Presumably transfer to local authority accommodation under other provisions in the Act would be considered.

Transfer of detained juveniles to local authority care

When the police keep a juvenile in custody after charge, they may transfer the young person to local authority care if s/he is not released. Equally, they may decide to keep the young person in their own custody. The original provisions of the Act and Codes have been the subject of much debate and argument, with the police reluctant to transfer to local authority care in some situations. This area of disagreement was tested out in the courts in R v. Chief Constable of Cambridgeshire *ex parte* M., High Court, 1990, and the court's decision led to a revision of the original provisions, a change enacted in section 59 of the Criminal Justice Act 1991. This confirms the position that it is a decision for the police, after discussion with the local social services department, about such a transfer, based on certain statutory criteria. Originally, the intention of Parliament was that such transfers should only be refused when, for example, weather conditions were too severe, or if there was a social workers' strike. However, the Cambridgeshire decision gave case law authority to the view that the police could decide on other criteria, which, in a more muted form, is contained within the Criminal Justice Act 1991.

The Cambridgeshire decision concerned the continued detention in a police station of a juvenile under section 38(6) of PACE because the custody officer thought the local authority should provide secure accommodation for the juvenile since otherwise the juvenile might interfere with the administration of justice: the juvenile was already in care and placed in the local authority's own residential care, whereas the local authority proposed to return him to his residential unit. The High Court rejected the view that the juvenile had been wrongfully imprisoned, as the judge considered that if the custody officer had allowed the transfer it would have effectively negated the custody officer's decision to refuse bail. The decision emphasised that the detainee remain in police detention although in local authority accommodation. (Regina v. Chief Constable of Cambridgeshire, *ex parte* M.; Queen's Bench Division; 1990; reported in *The Weekly Law Reports*, Part 19, 24 May 1991.)

The changes to section 38, subsections 6 and 6A of PACE, concerning the duties of the custody officer after charge, are made by section 59 of the Criminal Justice Act 1991. The new subsections are as follows:

6   *Where a custody officer authorises an arrested juvenile to be kept in police detention under subsection (1) above, the custody officer shall, unless he certifies :*

   (a)   that, by reason of such circumstances as are specified in the certificate, it is impracticable for him to do so; or

   (b)   in the case of an arrested juvenile who has attained the age of 12 years, that no secure accommodation is available and that keeping him in other local authority accommodation would not be adequate to protect the public from serious harm from him, secure that the arrested juvenile is moved to local authority accommodation

6A   *In this section 'local authority accommodation' means accommodation provided by or on behalf of a local authority (within the meaning of the Children Act 1989);*

   "secure accommodation" means accommodation provided for the purposes of restricting liberty;

   "sexual offence" and "violent offence" have the same meanings as in Part 1 of the Criminal Justice Act 1991;

and any reference, in relation to an arrested juvenile
charged with a violent or sexual offence, to protecting
the public from serious harm from him shall be
construed as a reference to protecting members of the
public from death or serious personal injury, whether
physical or psychological, occasioned by further such
offences committed by him.

The age in 6(b) above was originally 15, but changed to 12 by the 1994 Criminal Justice and Public Order Act.

This effectively means that the custody officer can decide on the transfer to local authority care, depending on the nature of the offence, and what accommodation the local authority offers. With the detainee's solicitor social workers will want to argue for the option that will remove the detainee from police cells, as it is clear the legislation, and good practice require this.

(See also Chapter 6, 'Issues of release of juveniles after charge and transfer to local authority care'.)

CONTINUED DETENTION BEFORE CHARGE

The review officer is responsible for determining if a detainee's continued detention continues to be necessary at regular intervals. For anyone called as an appropriate adult, part of their role in ensuring proper treatment is to check that the limits of detention are kept to, and reviews of detention are carried out properly.

A new requirement in the 1991 Codes is that, at each review of detention, the detainee must be reminded of his/her right to free legal advice (COP, C, 6.5 and 15.3) by the custody officer, who will record this in the custody record. The 1995 Codes state that whilst the Codes' provisions cover those taken to police stations under sections 135 and 136 of the Mental Health Act 1983, reviews of detention do not apply to those in these groups (COP, C, 1.10).

The appropriate adult should liaise with the review officer where there appears to be a breach of the Act or the Codes in terms of time limits and/or manner in which the review is carried out. This review officer will be of the rank of superintendent or above (PACE, s.40).

Periods of review will be at the following intervals:

    (a) Not later than six hours after the detention was first authorised;

    (b) Not later than nine hours after the first;

    (c) Subsequent reviews at intervals of not more than nine hours. (s.40(3) PACE)

If a person is questioned in hospital, on the way to or from it, the period concerned counts towards the total time permitted (COP, C, NOG, 14A).

Postponement of reviews may only take place if it is not practicable at the latest time specified for the review, or if the review officer is satisfied that an interruption of the questioning would prejudice the investigation; or if a review officer is not readily available (PACE, s. 40(4)).

Reasons for all decisions concerning reviews, and any delays, will be recorded on the custody record, and communicated to the detainee (s.40 (7) PACE, plus COP, C, 15.4, and 15.6).

Before determining whether to authorise a person's continued detention, the review officer shall:

    (a) give the detained person, (unless s/he is likely to be asleep, when the review should be brought forward), or

    (b) her/his solicitor representing her/him, or

    (c) the appropriate adult, if s/he is available or

    (d) other persons having an interest in his/her welfare,

an opportunity to make representations to him/her unless the detainee's behaviour or condition is unfit (s.40, 12-14, PACE, and COP, C, 15.1 and 15.2). Those specified in (c) and (d) were new inclusions in the 1991 codes, and continued in the 1995 Codes.

A person may not be kept in police custody for more than 24 hours without being charged unless an officer of at least the rank of superintendent or above responsible for the police station at which the person is detained has reasonable grounds for believing that

(a) it is necessary to secure or preserve evidence relating to an offence for which the detainee is under arrest, or to obtain such evidence by questioning him;

(b) an offence for which s/he is under arrest is a serious arrestable offence; and

(c) the investigation is being conducted diligently and expeditiously.

In these circumstances, detention may be authorised for up to 36 hours (s.42(1) PACE). The reviewing officer need not necessarily be at the police station where the detainee is held; discussion and permission may take place over the telephone for reviews up to 24 hours, but reviews at which authorisation longer than this period are considered, under Section 42 of the Act, should have the review officer there in person (COP, C, NOG, 15C).

If the social worker is in any doubt about the grounds, advice should be sought from a solicitor.

A 'serious arrestable offence' is defined in section 116 of PACE. Murder, manslaughter, causing death by reckless driving, incest with a girl under 13, buggery without consent or with a boy under 16, and rape, for example, are always in this category.

Any arrestable offence may, however, be treated as serious if it could lead to one of several consequences; e.g. serious interference with the investigation of an offence, serious injury or financial loss to any person. Full details are given in section 116, and associated schedule 5, of the Police and Criminal Evidence Act 1984.

The officer shall give the detainee or his/her legal representative, except where the detainee is considered unfit to do so because of her/his condition or behaviour, the opportunity to make representations about continued detention (s.42(7) and s.42 (8) PACE). A new provision of the 1991 codes and continued in the 1995 Codes was that the appropriate adult, if available at the time, or other persons having an interest in the detainee's welfare, may also make representations (COP, C, 15.1 and 15.2).

Where further detention is authorised, the detainee will be informed of the grounds, and these will be recorded on the custody record (s.42(9) PACE).

In any event, the detainee will be released with or without bail after 36 hours, unless:

(a) *s/he has been charged with an offence;*

(b) *her/his continued detention is authorised by a magistrate's court as laid down by section 43 of PACE (s.42, PACE). In this instance, the detainee should be told of the grounds for the police submission to the court in writing, and have access to legal representation;*

(c) *the Prevention of Terrorism (Temporary Provisions) Act 1989 applies, when the time limit is 48 hours before the police have to go to court.*

The 24 hour and 36 hour limits are operable from what the Act terms the 'relevant time'. Calculating this can be a complex task, involving such issues as transfers between police stations, and at what time the detainee was officially designated as having been detained. Always consult section 41 of PACE if there are any doubts: the Act will be available at police stations, although it is only the Codes of Practice which the police are required by law to make available.

Detention after charging a juvenile is permitted if the custody officer believes this would be in his/her best interests (s,38(1b) PACE).

Within these parameters, if a detainee is not charged, s/he should be released from custody, with or without bail, unless the custody officer says the detention is necessary because s/he has 'reasonable grounds for believing that his detention without being charged is necessary to secure or preserve evidence by questioning him.' (PACE, s. 37(2)).

GIVING CONSENT TO POLICE ACTIONS

Identification of persons by police officers

As in the codes covering interviews appropriate adults and interpreters have a role in identification procedures, and are set out in Code D.

(a) *If an officer has any suspicion, or is told in good faith, that a person of any age may be suffering from mental disorder or is mentally handicapped, or mentally incapable of understanding the significance of*

> *questions put to him or his replies, then that person*
> *shall be treated as a mentally disordered or mentally*
> *handicapped person for the purposes of this code.*
> *(COP, D, 1.3)*

> (b) *If anyone appears to be under the age of 17 then he*
> *shall be treated as a juvenile, for the purposes of this*
> *code in the absence of clear evidence to show that he*
> *is older. (COP, D, 1.4)*

> (c) *If a person appears to be blind or seriously visually*
> *handicapped, deaf, unable to read, unable to speak, or*
> *has difficulty orally because of a speech impediment*
> *he should be treated as such for the purposes of this*
> *code in the absence of clear evidence to the contrary.*
> *(COP, D, 1.5)*

The 'appropriate adult' for the different groups has the same definition and provisions as for Code C on interviewing procedures (see Chapter 3) (COP, D, 1.6, 1.14 and NOG 1A, 1B, 1C, 1D, and 1H).

Those reading documents and acting as interpreters are given similar guidance as for Code C on interviewing in section 1.11, 1.12, 1.13, and NOG 1F.

The forms of identification are:

• identity parades;

• confrontation by a witness;

• group identifications;

• video films;

If the appropriate adult finds him/herself in a situation where the detainee is to be put forward for forms of identification, s/he should always involve a solicitor, and as far as possible ensure, that relatives, especially of a juvenile, should be aware of what is happening, and have a chance to attend.

In the case of any procedure requiring a suspect's consent, the consent of a person who is mentally disordered or mentally handicapped is only valid if given in the presence of the appropriate adult; in the case of a juvenile the consent of his parent or guardian is required as well as his own (unless he is under 14, in which case the consent of his parent or guardian is sufficient in its own right) (COP, D, 1.11, and NOG 1E). However where a young person is accommodated, the parent/guardian would seem still to retain this right. Such consent is referred to as 'appropriate consent'.

> *In the case of a person who is blind or seriously visually handicapped or unable to read, the custody officer should ensure that his solicitor, relative or the appropriate adult or some other person likely to take an interest in him (and not involved in the investigation) is available to help in checking any documentation. Where this code requires written consent or signification, then the person who is assisting may be asked to sign instead if the detained person so wishes. (COP, D, 1.12)*

The role of the appropriate adult in these procedures, then, is to ensure that the detainee understands the processes that are taking place, the consequences of them, and to advise the detainee about these, including free legal advice if not already obtained. This is further confirmed by the following two sections:

> *In the case of any procedure requiring information to be given to or sought from a suspect, it must be given or sought in the presence of the appropriate adult if the suspect is mentally disordered, mentally handicapped, or a juvenile. If the appropriate adult is not present when the information is first given or sought, the procedure must be repeated in his presence when he arrives. If the suspect appears to be deaf or there is doubt about his hearing or speaking ability or ability to understand English, and the officer cannot establish effective communication, the information must be given or sought through an interpreter.' (COP, D, 1.13)*

> *Any procedure in this code involving the participation of a person (whether as a suspect or a witness) who is mentally disordered, mentally handicapped, or a juvenile must take place in the presence of the appropriate adult; but the adult must not be allowed to prompt any identification of a suspect by a witness. (COP, D, 1.14)*

These guidelines will not attempt to set out in detail all the requirements and powers concerning identification. Suffice it to say that if the situation arises, section 2 of code D, and Annexes A, B, and C, of code D should be consulted, and a solicitor called if one has not been called already. Several points are, however, worthy of note:

1 An identification officer, who will be of at least the rank of inspector, and who is not involved in the investigation of the case, will be responsible for the arrangements (COP, D, 2.2).

2 A suspect may refuse to take part in an identification parade, in which case arrangements will be made to allow the witness to see him/her in a group of people (COP, D, 2.6); if this happens, the suspect will be asked for his/her consent to this; if s/he refuses, the identification officer may proceed anyway (COP, D, 2.8).

3 The detainee must be given a written notice, which the detainee will be asked to sign to say whether s/he will cooperate or not; this notice will state (and which must also be explained verbally) the terms of the parade, group identification, or the making of a video film (COP, D, 2.15 and 2.16). This will include the facts that s/he may refuse, but that this may lead to a confrontation by a witness, and refusal may be given in evidence in any subsequent trial, and police may proceed covertly without his consent or make other arrangements to test whether a witness identifies him; and that juveniles, and those who are mentally disordered or who are mentally handicapped are subject to special arrangements; and that s/he is entitled to free legal advice.

A suspect must also have reasonable opportunity to have a solicitor or a friend present (COP, D, Annex A, (1)). Once a parade has been formed, all subsequent events have to be witnessed by an interpreter, solicitor, friend, or appropriate adult (COP, D, Annex A (7)).

Confrontation by a witness can only take place in the presence of the suspect's solicitor, interpreter, or friend, unless this would cause unreasonable delay (COP, D, Annex C, (3) and (4)).

PHOTOGRAPHS OF THE DETAINEE (AND COMPUTER IMAGES)

'Appropriate consent' (see page 73) is needed for the taking of photographs of detainees who are mentally disordered, mentally handicapped, those mentally incapable of understanding and juveniles.

Written consent is required in the presence of the appropriate adult, and the detainee must have been told of the reasons for taking the photograph, and that it will be destroyed if s/he is not prosecuted of the offence and cleared of it, or if s/he is not prosecuted (unless s/he admits the offence and is cautioned for it.) S/he must be told that s/he may witness the destruction of the photographs or be provided with a certificate confirming their destruction if s/he applies within 5 days of being cleared, or of being informed that no prosecution will take place.

An appropriate adult acting as appropriate adult cannot give consent to the photographing of a detainee who is a juvenile (COP, D, 1.11 and NOG 1E), nor to a mentally disordered or mentally handicapped person being photographed, although in the latter circumstance s/he has to be present when the person is asked for consent.

In some circumstances, a social worker acting as an appropriate adult for a juvenile on a care order can give consent.

The appropriate adult will wish to ensure that the detainee is aware that if s/he agrees to a caution, the photograph can be retained.

Photographs can only be taken without consent where a person is:

• arrested at the same time as other persons, or at a time when it is likely that other persons will be arrested, and the photograph is necessary to establish who was arrested, at what time, and at what place;

• charged with or reported for a recordable offence and has not yet been released or brought before a court. Recordable offences in the code mean those offences for which convictions are recorded in national police records (see COP, D, NOG, 3A, and section 27(4) of PACE) or

• s/he is convicted of such an offence and his/her photograph is not already on record as a result of the two items above. There is no power of arrest to take a photograph in the pursuance of this provision (COP, D, 4.2).

Force may not be used by the police to take a photograph (COP, D. 4.3).

A written record of reasons for photographing without consent should be made as soon as possible, and of the destruction of any photographs (COP, D, 4.5).

FINGERPRINTING AND PALMPRINTING OF THE DETAINEE

Unlike photographs, fingerprints and palmprints can be taken with 'reasonable' force from someone over 10 years of age (COP, D, 3.2 and 3.6, and s.61, PACE), if consent from the parent or guardian is unforthcoming. A social worker acting as an appropriate adult for a juvenile cannot give this consent; s/he may only give it if s/he works for a local authority or voluntary organisation with whom a young person is 'in Care' (COP, D, NOG 1E). Presumably the term 'in care' may also refer to a young person who is accommodated, but this in not clear. It would seem good practice not to give consent where the young person is not subject to a court order, as the parents/guardians still retain full parental authority and responsibility in these circumstances under the Children Act, 1989.

Forcible fingerprinting can take place when:

1   *An officer of at least the rank of superintendent authorises it; or if s/he has been charged with a recordable offence or informed that s/he will be reported for such an offence; and s/he has not had fingerprints taken in the course of the investigation of the offence by police;*

2   *The superintendent may only give an authorisation to take the fingerprints without appropriate consent if s/he has reasonable grounds for suspecting involvement of the person whose fingerprints are to be taken in a criminal offence; and for believing that his/her finger prints will tend to confirm or disprove his/her involvement. (PACE, s.61)*

3   *If finger or palmprints are taken without consent, reasons for doing so must be recorded as soon as possible. (COP, D, 3.7)*

Any person's fingerprints may be taken without the appropriate consent if s/he has been convicted of a recordable offence (section 61 of PACE does not apply to detainees under the immigration or terrorism acts) (PACE, s.61(6)). If a person:

(a) *Has been convicted of a recordable offence;*

(b) Has not at any time been in police detention for the offence; and has not had her/his fingerprints taken in the course of the investigation of the offence by the police; or since the conviction, any constable may at any time not later than one month after the date of the conviction require him/her to attend a police station in order that his/her fingerprints may be taken. Such a requirement shall give the person a period of at least seven days within which s/he must attend, and may direct him/her to so attend at a specified time of day or between specified times of day. Any constable may arrest without warrant a person who has failed to comply with the requirement of this section. (PACE, s.27)

Within 5 days of being told s/he is not to be charged or is cleared, s/he has the right to witness their destruction if s/he requests this (COP, D, 3.1). 'When fingerprints are destroyed, access to relevant computer data shall be made impossible as soon as it is practicable to do so' (COP, D, 3.5) and a record of this made (COP, D, 3.7). If the detainee agrees to a caution, this means s/he has admitted the offence, and the fingerprints can be retained.

STRIP SEARCHES, INTIMATE AND NON-INTIMATE BODY SEARCHES AND BODY SAMPLES

A written record must be made by the custody officer of all the property a detained person has on them at the point of their arrest at the police station, or on his/her arrival at the police station, either after his/her arrest, or as an order of the court (PACE, s.54). The detainee may be searched under PACE or the Mental Health Act 1983, sections 135 or 136, to ascertain what property s/he has, or under PACE, what property s/he might have acquired for an unlawful or harmful purpose while in custody, although intimate searches or removal of more than outer clothing is covered by Annex A of Code C (see below). Not every person has to be searched (COP, C, NOG,4A). See section 4 of COP C for full details of taking and safeguarding of detainee's property.

Strip searches

Strip searches may only be carried out by an officer of the same sex (COP, C, Annex A, paragraph 6) and involves a search involving the removal of more than outer clothing. 'No person of the opposite sex who is not a medical practitioner or nurse shall be present, nor shall anyone else whose presence is unnecessary but a minimum of 2 people, other than the person being searched must be present.' (COP, C, Annex A, paragraph 6).

The strip search may only take place if the custody officer considers it necessary to remove an article which the detained person would not be allowed to keep (COP, C, Annex A, paragraph 10). This is in effect nearly everything; though clothing and personal effects can only be seized if the police have reason to believe they may be evidence relating to an offence by the person, or the person might injure him/herself or others, attempt to escape, interfere with evidence, or damage property with them (PACE, s.54(4), and COP, C, 4.2 and 4.3). Reasons for seizure of property will be given to the detainee except where s/he is violent or likely to be violent or is incapable of understanding what is being said to her/him.

Such a search does not require 'appropriate consent', and is on the authority of the custody officer, who will record the reasons for the search and its results (COP, C, Annex A, paragraph 7). If it was carried out by a police officer, and not a qualified person, reasons for this must be recorded (COP, C, Annex A, paragraph 8).

Intimate body searches

These searches of certain body orifices (see PACE s.55) can be legally authorised by an officer of at least the rank of superintendent when s/he has reasonable grounds for believing that a person has been arrested, and being in police detention, may have concealed on him or her anything which could be used to cause physical injury to him/herself or others, and s/he might use it while in police detention, or in the custody of the court. Such a search should take place only at a hospital, surgery, other medical premises or police station (COP, C, Annex A, paragraph 4).

The other purpose for which an intimate body search may be authorised is if the superintendent (or above) believes a Class A drug is concealed on the person and the person was in possession of it with the appropriate criminal intent before his/her arrest (PACE, s.55(1), and COP, C, Annex A, paragraph 1).

The officer has to believe that the search is needed because anything the detainee is suspected of concealing cannot be found without it, for example if the detainee refuses it when asked (as s/he should have been) (PACE, s.55(2)).

An intimate search which is only a Class A drug offence search shall be by way of examination by a suitably qualified person only, a nurse or doctor but not a police officer, and shall only take place at a hospital, surgery, or other medical premises, not at a police station. (PACE, s.55(4) and (9), and COP, C, Annex A, paragraph 3 and 4).

Other types of intimate body strip searches can also only be carried out by a suitably qualified person unless the superintendent considers this is not practicable. In that instance, a constable should carry out the search, but this may only be a constable of the same sex; no one of the opposite sex should be present, nor anyone whose presence is unnecessary (PACE, s.55(5),(6),(7), and COP, C, Annex A, paragraphs 3 and 6). If an intimate search (not for Class A drugs) is carried out by a police officer, the reasons why must be recorded (COP, C, Annex A, paragraph 8).

As soon as possible after such an intimate search, the custody officer will record which parts of the body were searched, and by whom, who was present, the reasons for it and results (COP, C, Annex A, paragraph 7 and PACE, s.55(10)). The grounds for seizing anything found are the same as for those in strip searches (see page 77).

Vulnerable groups and intimate body searches

The 1985 Codes state that

> *An intimate search at a police station of a juvenile or a mentally disordered or mentally handicapped person may take place only in the presence of an appropriate adult of the same sex [and a new provision added to this by the 1991 and 1995 Codes goes on] unless the person specifically requests the presence of a particular adult of the opposite sex who is readily available. In the case of a juvenile, the search may take place in the absence of the appropriate adult only if the juvenile signifies in the presence of the appropriate adult that he prefers the search to be done in his absence, and the appropriate adult agrees. A record shall be made of the*

juvenile's decision and signed by the appropriate adult.
(COP, C, Annex A, Note 5)

Where an intimate search or strip search, is taking place, 'no person of the opposite sex who is not a medical practitioner or nurse shall be present nor shall anyone whose presence is unnecessary.' (COP, C, Annex A, Note 6).

Appropriate adults will want to consider very carefully whether they remain present at such searches. If a person wants the appropriate adult to be present because of fears or concerns, then this will be appropriate. If, however, the detainee is in regular contact with the appropriate adult or is likely to be, the effect on that person's attitude to their remaining present at such searches may compromise future contact. The appropriate adult should respect the detainee's wishes over this. While paragraph 5, Annex A of Code C, quoted above, gives the detainee the right to ask for a particular adult of either sex if s/he is readily available, and this should be respected, (e.g. if the detainee asks for his/her own social worker who is available), in other circumstances the appropriate adult should discuss with the detainee, in private if this would be easier, whether s/he wishes not to have an appropriate adult present. Alternatively if s/he wishes to have an appropriate adult who is of the same sex, and the latter is not of that sex, the social worker should, where possible, call in a colleague of the same sex as the detainee.

Appropriate adults should ensure that the privacy intended by the Act and Codes is strictly adhered to, given the psychological and legal effects of such a search. If it is not adhered to the appropriate adult should ensure that s/he asks for an entry in the custody record to be made, and makes contact with the solicitor representing the detainee to ensure that they are aware of this.

Taking of body samples

There are two types of body sample under the Act:

> *(a) non-intimate body samples are samples of hair (other*
> *than pubic hair), a nail cutting or scraping from*
> *beneath a nail, a footprint or impression from any part*
> *of the person's body other than a part of his/her hand,*
> *or a swab taken from any part of a person's body*
> *other than the body orifices. (PACE, s.65)*

Taking of these samples has to have 'appropriate consent' (see page 73) in writing. This can be over-ruled by an officer of at least the rank of superintendent where s/he believes the detainee may have committed a serious arrestable offence (see page 70), and that the sample will tend to confirm or disprove the detainee's involvement (COP,D, 5.4 and PACE s.63(2,3,4)). 'Reasonable force' can be used if the superintendent agrees (COP, D, 5.6). Even if the appropriate consent is given, an officer of the rank of inspector or above must agree to it on the same grounds.

b)   *Intimate samples and dental impressions are samples of blood, semen, or any other tissue, fluid, urine, saliva, pubic hair, or a swab taken from a body orifice. (PACE, s.65)*

These may be taken when authorised by an officer of at least the rank of superintendent and where the appropriate consent is given (see page 73) in writing, and where the superintendent believes the detaince may have committed a serious arrestable offence, and the body sample will tend to confirm or disprove the detainee's involvement (PACE, s.62, and COP, D, 5.1).

Any intimate body sample, except urine, must be taken only by a registered medical practitioner or dental practitioner as appropriate. (PACE, s.62(9), and COP, D, 5.3).

If 'appropriate consent' is withheld without 'good cause... (a court) ... may draw such inferences from the refusal as appears proper; and the refusal may, on the basis of such inferences, be treated as, or as capable of amounting to, corroboration of any evidence against the person in relation to which the refusal is material.' (PACE, s.62(10)).

The detainee should be warned that this is the case, and that refusal may be treated in any proceedings against him/her as corroborating relevant prosecution evidence (COP, D, 5.2, and NOG 5A). It is clear that in these circumstances the social worker will need to have access to legal advice by way of means outlined earlier (page 44), as the actual process of taking such samples has clear implications not only for the social worker's present and subsequent roles, but also in terms of the legal process itself. Legal advice is therefore essential in such situations.

5 TAPE RECORDING OF INTERVIEWS

Tape recording of interviews is now standard and is an important development as it is the recordings themselves or transcripts of them which are widely used by the Crown Prosecution Service and other parts of the justice system in making judgements about guilt and culpability. Tape recording the interview should minimise the risk of practices which are prejudicial against detainee's rights and fair interviews. It does require the appropriate adult to be aware of the processes involved, and his/her role, as events seem to happen more quickly and more formally in tape recorded interviews. It is also particularly important that the appropriate adult ensures that no unfair practices, as discussed in earlier chapters take place when the tape recorder is switched off, or during breaks in the tape recording. If the appropriate adult observes any practices which seem to be in breach of the Codes and/or Act, it is her/his duty to draw this to the attention of the interviewing officer, and if not satisfied with his/her response, then to bring it to the attention of the custody officer who is responsible for the treatment of the detainee under the Act and Codes. The general provisions set out in these guidelines also apply to taped interviews, and section 1.3 of the Codes states that 'Nothing in this code shall be taken as detracting in any way from the requirements of the Code of Practice for the Detention, Treatment, and Questioning of Persons by Police Officers.' (COP, E, 1.3).

The code is issued under PACE s.60(1)(a).

Failure of police officers to follow the Code in areas where they are required to do so can render him/her liable to disciplinary proceedings under PACE s.67(8), unless such proceedings are precluded by PACE, s.104. PACE. s.67(10) means that not following the Code does not of itself render him/her liable to criminal or civil proceedings, and has the same status in such proceedings as the other Codes, as do the Notes of Guidance and the Annexes (see page 8).

As with the other Codes, Code E must be readily available for detainees and the public at police stations designated to hold detainees. Since 1995, it is now part of the booklet containing the other Codes.

WHEN TAPE RECORDINGS WILL BE USED

The whole of each interview will be taped, including the taking and reading back of any statement (COP, E, 3.5).

Apart from interviews with detainees held under the Prevention of Terrorism (Temporary Provisions) Act 1989, or the Official Secrets Act 1911, 'tape recording shall be used at police stations for any interview:

> *(a) with a person who has been cautioned in accordance with section 10 of code C in respect of an indictable offence (including an offence triable either way) (COP, E, 3.1), although this does not preclude tape recording of interviews where someone is cautioned for other type of offences (COP, E, NOG, 3A), but also see paragraph 12.3 of code C, where someone is unfit through drink or drugs. (COP, E, NOG, 3B)*

> *(b) which takes place as a result of a police officer exceptionally putting further questions to a suspect about an offence described in sub-paragraph a) above after he has been charged with, or informed he may be prosecuted for, that offence. (COP, E, 3.1)*

> *(c) in which a police officer wishes to bring to the notice of a person, after he has been charged with, or informed he may be prosecuted for an offence described in sub-paragraph (a) above, any written statement made by another person, or the content of an interview with another person.' (COP, E, 3.1)*

Note of Guidance 3D, code E, states that procedures by which this will happen are set out in paragraph 16.4 of code C, and that one method of doing this is by playing a tape recording of the other person's interview. If someone attending the police station voluntarily is subsequently cautioned, the interview will then be taped, unless paragraph 3.3 applies.

When an interview need not be tape recorded

The custody officer may authorise the interviewing officer not to tape record the interview if the recording equipment is not available, and if s/he considers it would cause unreasonable delay to wait for the problem to be overcome where it is clear from the outset that no prosecution will ensue (COP, E, 3.3).

If there is pressure on resources for tape recording interviews, priority should be given to those suspected of more serious offences (COP, E, NOG 3J).

If during the course of the interview it becomes clear that an offence under the Prevention of Terrorism (Temporary Provisions) Act 1989 may have been committed by the detainee, the tape recorder should be switched off (COP, E, NOG 3G and 3H).

If the suspect indicates s/he wishes to tell the officer of matters not directly connected with the offence for which s/he is suspected but is unwilling for them to be taped, s/he will be given the opportunity to tell the police about these matters at the end of the interview (COP, E, 4.7).

THE ARRANGEMENTS FOR THE INTERVIEW

As soon as the suspect is brought into the interview room, the police officer will load the tape recorder with previously unused tapes and set it to record in the sight of the suspect. The tapes must be seen to be unwrapped by the suspect (COP, E, 4.1). The officer will then tell the suspect formally about the tape recording, and say

- that the interview is being tape recorded;
- his name, rank, and those of any other officers present, except in the case of terrorist offences;
- the name of the suspect, of any other party present, e.g. solicitor, and/or appropriate adult. The interviewing officer may ask each person present to identify themselves. Social workers and others acting as appropriate adults should give their name, job title or status (e.g. volunteer, sessional worker), and their agency's contact address (not their home address);
- the date, time of commencement and place of the interview;
- that the suspect will be given a notice about what will happen to the tapes (COP, E, 4.2).

The police officer shall give the new standard caution as set out in Chapter 3. Minor deviations from this do not breach the Code. If it seems the detainee does not understand or appreciate the significance of the caution, the interviewing officer should explain it in his/her own words, and explain further if needs be (COP, E, 4.3, and NOG, 4C). The social worker should check directly with the detainee that s/he does understand the implications of the caution, and only allow the interview to continue when s/he is happy that the detainee does understand.

If the detainee is 'deaf or there is doubt about his hearing ability', the interviewing officer should make a contemporaneous note of the interview in line with Code C requirements (see page 63 of this guide) (COP, E, 4.4 and NOG 4E and 4F).

OBJECTIONS AND COMPLAINTS BY THE DETAINEE

If the detainee objects to the interview being tape recorded at the outset of, during, or in a break from the interview, the officer should state that the objections will be recorded on the tape as the Codes require. Once this has been done, or the detainee refuses to state the reasons for the objections, the officer will then give her/his reasons for doing so, and turn the tape off. A written record will then be made as required in section 11 of Code C (see page 7). However, if the officer 'reasonably considers that he may proceed to put questions to the suspect with the tape recorder still on, he may do so,' though the officer should bear in mind that a decision to continue recording against the detainee's wishes may be commented upon in court (COP, E, 4.5, and NOG 4G).

If the person makes a complaint during the course of an interview, or if the appropriate adult does so, the officer shall act in accordance with the provisions of Code C, 12.8 (see page 61). The tape recorder should be left running to record the discussion with the custody officer, and the interviewing officer may then continue or cease tape recording under an inspector's instruction, unless it is a matter not to do with Codes C or E (COP, C, 9.1 and COP, E, NOG 4H and 4J).

BREAKS IN THE INTERVIEW

When a break is to be taken and the interview room vacated by the suspect, this will be recorded on the tape, along with the time, and the reason for the break. The tapes will then be removed from the recorder and the same procedures as for ending an interview followed (see below) (COP, E, 4.9).

If there is to be a short break, and both the suspect and the police are to remain in the interview room, the fact of the break, the time and the reasons for it will be recorded on the tape. The recorder may then be switched off, with no need to remove the tapes. On recommencement of the interview the time of this will be recorded on the tape (COP, E, 4.10).

When someone is being interviewed under caution, the officer must ensure the detainee realises s/he is still under caution, and repeat this if there is any doubt, as the officer may have to convince a court the detainee was aware s/he was still under caution (COP, E, NOG 4K). The officer may recount on the tape what happened during the break and ask the detainee to confirm this as s/he may need to justify to a court what did happen (COP, E, NOG, 4L). The appropriate adult should therefore ensure it is an accurate description of events.

If a tape should break, the machine fail, or the tapes are removed for any other reason during the interview, the appropriate adult should check with the Code of Practice E on tape recording, sections 4.12 and 4.13 and NOG 4M, to ensure that the proper procedures have been followed.

After the interview

The interviewing officer should write the time, duration and date of the interview in his/her notebook, that it was recorded on tape, and the identification number of the master tape (COP, E, 5.1).

If proceedings follow, the officer shall prepare a written record of the interview which will be signed by the officer. The interview record shall be exhibited to any written statement prepared by the officer (COP, E, 5.3). For further details of what happens to the tapes if the matter proceeds to court, although not directly relevant to the role of the appropriate adult see COP, E, paragraphs 6.1 to 6.3.

Where no proceedings follow

The tapes must still be kept securely (COP, E, 6.1 and NOG 6A). It is the responsibility of the chief officer of police to establish arrangements for the breaking of the seal of the master tape (see below), if this is deemed necessary. Once applied, the tape should not have its seal broken, except with her/his permission.

RECORDING AND SEALING OF MASTER TAPES

The purpose of recording interviews is to ensure that independent scrutiny of interviews can take place once they have taken place, and sealing of tapes in the presence of the detainee is a vital part of this process. Before this can be done, the detainee shall be offered the chance to clarify or add anything s/he may wish (COP, E, 4.14). Then the time will be recorded and the tape recorder switched off. 'The master tape shall be sealed, with a master tape label and treated as an exhibit in accordance with the force standing orders. The police officer shall sign the label and ask the suspect and any third party present, to sign it also. If any of these refuse to sign, an officer of at least the rank of inspector will be called into the interview room to sign it. The detainee will then be handed a notice explaining what use will be made of the tapes, and the arrangements for access to it.' (COP, E, 4.15, 4.16).

THE APPROPRIATE ADULT'S ROLE

If the appropriate adult believes that any of the provisions of the Codes or Act have been breached, s/he should bring this to the attention of the interviewing officer, while the tape is running. If the appropriate adult is dissatisfied with the response, s/he should bring the matter to the attention of the custody officer (section 12.8 of Code C, and see page 61 of this guide). Remember that all the provisions of Code C, set out earlier in this guide, still cover tape recorded interviews (COP, E, 1.3). If at the end of the interview, the appropriate adult has any concerns about the interview or what has happened during it, s/he should state these clearly on the tape at the time. As with all such statements or interventions, the appropriate adult should state who s/he is, and why s/he is making the intervention. S/he should also make a written record of the contents of it at the time, as this may be the basis of either a complaint about police behaviour, or be used in any subsequent Crown Prosecution proceedings or court hearings.

ACCESS TO THE TAPE AFTER THE INTERVIEW

Although it is not stated explicitly in Code E, the detainee, her/his solicitor and, presumably, the appropriate adult should have access to the working copy of the tape, or the transcript of it in the same way as for custody records (see page 64). The master tape is kept sealed, in the possession of the police under strict criteria set out in COP, E, 6.1 and NOG 6A. The seal of the master tape cannot be broken by the police except on the authority of, and in the presence of a representative of the Crown Prosecution Service. The detainee and his/her solicitor must be informed of this action and given the opportunity to be present, and to re-seal the tape (COP, E, 6.2 and NOG 6B and 6C).

6   ISSUES OF RELEASE OF JUVENILES AFTER CHARGE AND TRANSFER TO LOCAL AUTHORITY CARE AFTER CHARGE

The appropriate adult who is not a social worker employed by a local authority will not become embroiled in this difficult area. Where s/he is so employed as a social worker, s/he has a duty to liaise with colleagues in his/her department to ensure that proper details are made available, and that proper procedures are put into place when a juvenile is transferred to their care. This chapter sets out the areas the social worker needs to take into account in such situations.

CHARGING AND RELEASING

On arrival at the Police Station, if a charge is not brought straight away, the detainee should be released, unless the custody officer believes that detention is necessary to secure or preserve evidence in relation to an offence for which s/he is under arrest, or to obtain such evidence by questioning (PACE, s.37 (2)).

In certain circumstances, the police will consider a formal caution. In this instance:

- the accused must admit the offence;
- the police must have evidence that they believe would gain a conviction in a court of law; and
- the police must be convinced that it will be in the public interest.

Do not see a caution as your client 'getting off'. A caution will be recorded on police records for future reference. It will almost certainly be brought up in court, and it will definitely be treated as a conviction if the young person offends again. Advise your client of the right to consult a solicitor; this may be particularly important where the issue of strength of police evidence is in doubt.

Once the detainee is charged he or she must be released with or without bail to appear in court, unless further detention is deemed necessary because the custody officer:

- cannot ascertain the detainee's name or address, or believes that those given are false;

- believes this is necessary for his/her own protection, or it is to prevent him/her from causing physical injury to any other person or from causing loss of or damage to property; or

- believes that the person arrested will fail to appear in court to answer bail, or that it is necessary to prevent the detainee from interfering with the administration of justice or investigation of an offence (PACE, s.38 (1a)).

In addition, a juvenile may be detained after charge if the custody officer believes that 'he ought to be detained in his own interests.' (PACE, s.38 (1b)).

Neither the Act nor the Codes nor the subsequent Government circulars clarify what these interests might be, and when the social services department is contacted, the social worker involved will want to know exactly what the reasons are likely to be, as this has implications for their role. He or she might want to investigate the reasons and take further action, for example, if there is a problem with the young person's family where a resolution might lead to bail and a return home, or to help in returning a juvenile to his/her family if they are detained a long way from home.

If further detention is authorised under this section, the reasons will be recorded in the custody record, and the detainee informed of these reasons (PACE, s.38 (3) (4)).

THE POLICE DUTY TO INFORM AND CONSULT THE LOCAL AUTHORITY

Where a custody officer authorises an arrested juvenile to be kept in police detention under sub-section 1 (of s.38) above, the custody officer shall, unless he certifies that it is impracticable to do so, make arrangements for the arrested juvenile to be taken into care of a local authority and

detained by the authority; and it shall be lawful to detain him
in pursuance of the arrangements. (PACE, s.38 (6))

If the police decide that a transfer to local authority care is impracticable, a certificate has to be made out authorising the detention in police custody which will 'be produced for the court before which he is first brought thereafter.' (PACE, s.38(7)).

There is no indication in official sources as to what may make the police decide to certify that it is impracticable to transfer a juvenile to local authority care. The only guidance is in section 59 of the Criminal Justice Act 1991 which amends s.38 (6) of PACE, see page 66, and Code C Note of Guidance 16B, and sections 16.6 and 16.9.

'Where a juvenile is charged with an offence and the custody officer authorises his continuing detention he must try to make arrangements for the juvenile to be taken into the care of the local authority to be detained pending appearance in court unless he certifies that it is impracticable to do so, or, in the case of a juvenile of at least 12 years of age, no secure accommodation is available and there is a risk of serious harm from that juvenile, in accordance with section 38 (6) of the Police and Criminal Evidence Act 1984' as amended by section 59 of the Criminal Justice Act 1991 and section 24 of the Criminal Justice and Public Order Act 1994 (COP, C, 16.6), 'the custody officer must record the reasons and make out a certificate to be produced before the court together with the juvenile.' (COP, C, 16.9). 'Neither a juvenile's behaviour nor the nature of the offence with which he is charged provides grounds for the custody officer to retain him in police custody rather than seek to arrange for his transfer to the care of the local authority.' The new 1995 Codes add: 'Similarly accommodation shall not make it impracticable for the custody officer to transfer him. The availability of secure accommodation is only a factor in relation to a juvenile aged 12 or over when the Local Authority would not be adequate to protect the public from serious harm from the juvenile. The obligation to transfer a juvenile to Local Authority accommodation applies as much to a juvenile charged during the daytime as it does to a juvenile held overnight, subject to a requirement to bring the juvenile before a court under section 46 of the PACE 1984, (COP, C, NOG 16B). This would seem to mean that in all situations, the custody officer must consult with the local authority. Only if s/he determines that the accommodation offered by the local authority is not suitable, which will normally be for reasons of suitability in terms of ensuring the young person is returned to court, will transfer not occur. If such negotiations do not take place and social services personnel become aware of this, they should take the issue up at an appropriately senior level with the police.

Such contact then places the local authority in the position where a decision has to be made about placing a young person when the police have contacted them.

THE DUTY OF THE LOCAL AUTHORITY

Good practice, and the social services department's duty to promote the welfare of young people, means that there should be ready access to local authority care, although no specific legal duty under the Act exists.

Social workers should check with those responsible within the authorities' decision-making processes concerning this, especially as such decisions are often needed outside office hours. For example: are local community homes used on a transfer to care? Is there another form of residential establishment? Are there foster homes? All these are vital elements for the planning concerning the transfer to local authority care, because there are certain specific duties on the local authority about producing the young person before the court again, and these duties have implications for the care of that young person. Social workers will also want to know what provisions are made for those mentioned who might receive the young person to have access to the guidelines and knowledge they will need to have in this situation. Will those carers know about the duties of the local authorities to produce the young person in court and the ramifications of this? Will they know that they are expected to allow all the legal rights of the young person as defined by the Codes of Practice, for example access to a solicitor? Will they know what to do if the young person goes missing, and how to go about deciding limitations of movement of the young person? The issues should be made clear to those carers.

The greatest clarity on the duties of the local authority comes in the relevant DHSS (as it then was) Circular 'L.A.C. (85) 18', available from Department of Health, Alexander Fleming House, Elephant and Castle, London SE1 6BY.

*Local authorities should ensure that adequate arrangements
are available for social services departments to be contacted
by the police out of normal working hours to ensure that
wherever possible, an arrested and detained juvenile is
passed into their care. (DHSS, LAC (85), 18) (see also s.21,
Children Act, 1989)*

*Section 39 (5) (of PACE) lays a duty on a local authority to
make available to an arrested juvenile who is in a local
authority's care under section 38 (6) (of PACE) such advice
and assistance as may be appropriate in the circumstances.
Local authorities should have regard to the Codes of
Practice, and in particular, the provisions relating to
detention, searching, and treatment of detained persons, to
ensure that a juvenile detained in care is treated no less
favourably than if s/he were detained by the police. (DHSS
(85) 18)*

The implications here are clear: there is a duty on local authorities to
ensure that all involved, appropriate adults, residential staff, foster
parents, have ready access to clear information about their duties to
the courts and to the young people. One way of doing this would be to
have readily available such guidelines as presented here, preferably
through a designated member of staff who has a full working
knowledge of the issues raised and can therefore act as adviser and
consultant.

SECURE ACCOMMODATION

The circular reminds local authorities that the police will have already
considered and rejected release from detention. It is still a matter for
the local authority to decide where to place the young person.

*If it is decided that the most suitable form of accommodation
is secure accommodation the juvenile may, for the time
being, be so accommodated, in which case the provisions of
section 21a of the Child Care Act 1980, or the Secure
Accommodation (2) Regulations 1983 do not apply. (DHSS
(85), 18, paragraph 5)*

Such a decision would need to be made at an appropriately senior level
in an organisation. The deprivation of someone's liberty in this context

is an extremely serious matter. Any such decision would have to be based upon the seriousness of an offence, and the likelihood of the young person attempting to abscond from care.

PRODUCING THE YOUNG PERSON IN COURT

Where a juvenile 'is detained by a local authority' under PACE s.38 (6), 'he shall be brought before a magistrates court in accordance with the provisions of this section.' (PACE, s.46 (1)) The social worker will want to ensure, details of the court appearance by way of liaison with police and the clerks to the justices locally. It is the local authority's duty to ensure the juvenile is produced in court, and a social worker in consultation with senior staff will want to make sure that proper arrangements are made for this, given the client's circumstances and any difficulties which can be anticipated; for example, do two staff need to be involved in transportation? Will the young person have adequate time before the court appearance to finalise details with the solicitor? As the detainee is still in police custody, negotiations may need to take place with the police to ensure that they are involved in plans for the transport of the young person to court.

CHILD CARE DUTIES OF A SOCIAL WORKER ACTING AS AN APPROPRIATE ADULT IN THE CASE OF A JUVENILE

There may on occasions be situations where the role of the appropriate adult and the role of the social worker appear to be in conflict. One such situation is where the social worker attends as an appropriate adult where parents or guardians may be refusing to have the young person home for some reason. If the social worker investigates fully before attending, as suggested in these guidelines, rifts in a young person's home situation may be alleviated sufficiently to avoid this, or he or she would discover the likelihood of refusal before a police interview takes place. The lines of communication to enable further negotiation of work will in any event have been opened, for use after the interview and would have allowed a period for initial anger and rejection towards the young person to subside. An appropriate adult who is not a local authority social worker may want to consult with the social services department in such circumstances.

If the police are not detaining the young person after charge, and parents/guardians are refusing to have him or her back, these channels of communication should be used to effect reconciliation if possible. Discussion about the nature of the offence (as opposed to parents'/guardians' fantasies), the attitude of the young person after charge, and getting the young person to talk directly, over the telephone and/or in person by taking him/her there, can be ways of effecting this.

The police may sometimes wish for a young person to be placed in local authority accommodation because of the family's initial rejection, or because they believe the young person has an unsuitable address, e.g. a squat or bed and breakfast address, or because of the reasons stated previously in this section. In these circumstances the social worker is involved in a full assessment of the situation, which may lead to the social worker negotiating on a young person's behalf regarding the suitability of their accommodation, arranging alternative suitable accommodation, e.g. a sympathetic landlady or hostel for someone over 16 years of age, or even a return home to a previously hostile family. It may eventually lead to accommodating the young person under the Children Act 1989, depending on the social work assessment, but not on the police assessment of the viability of anything the social worker arranges, as long as this does not conflict with police duties (PACE, s.38 (1a), PACE s.38 (1b) and 38(6)), previously outlined above. The latter will, however, be difficult for the police to justify if the social worker has made alternative arrangements.

In any event, the social worker should have made her/his role clear in relation to these matters of care if they seem a possibility and the young person has a right to know the powers and duties of any person attending the situation which can have a profound effect on their immediate, and possible long-term, future. This will also make the change of role from 'appropriate adult' to 'child care officer' easier for all concerned when and if it becomes necessary.

Local authority policy

The social worker will always want to ensure he or she is fully aware of any policies in the authority regarding their role in relation to care matters; these guidelines are presented as practice notes, and some authorities' policies may not always accord with them.

7 THE SEARCHING OF RESIDENTIAL HOMES, DAY CENTRES AND OTHER PREMISES BY THE POLICE

Police searches of residential homes and other establishments can only be carried out in prescribed circumstances, when certain criteria apply.

Staff and managers of such establishments will need to be familiar with the provisions of the Act in order to protect the legal rights of the whole of the resident group. These guidelines will be of particular interest to those working in young people's establishments, those caring for people who are mentally disordered or mentally handicapped, and to foster parents.

ACCESS TO PREMISES

There are two ways in which the police can gain access to premises:

(a) With a Warrant

This must be a warrant signed by a JP and the senior member of staff on duty should check that the warrant states:

(i)   the grounds for the application;

(ii)   specifies the premises which the police wish to enter and search;

(iii)   identifies as far as it is practicable the articles or persons to be sought. (PACE, s.15)

The warrant is valid for one occasion only which should be within one month of the date of issue. A copy of the warrant must be shown to the person in charge at the time and given to that person. The search should take place at a reasonable hour, unless it would frustrate the purpose of the search. The officer should identify him or herself, and if not in uniform, s/he should provide documentary evidence (PACE, s.16).

These checks could be of importance later in discussions with senior staff at the police station, if further clarification for the reason of the search is sought, or if there are queries about the way in which the search is carried out.

(b) *Access without a Warrant*

> *There are several grounds on which a police officer may demand entry to premises without a warrant:*

> (i)   *To search for a person who is subject to a warrant of arrest;*

> (ii) *A warrant of Commitment under the Magistrates Courts Act, s.76, 1980, exists, when the officer must produce the original warrant.*

> (iii) *To arrest a person for an arrestable offence. [An arrestable offence is defined in the Legal Action Group's Book, 'A Practitioner's Guide to the Police and Criminal Evidence Act, 1984', by Fiona Hargreaves and Howard Levenson.]*

> (iv) *Where there is an offensive weapon in a public place:*

> (v)   *To recapture an escapee;*

> (vi) *To save life or limb. (PACE s.17)*

There are also powers to enter and search any premises when:

> *A suspect was there at the time of or immediately prior to, arrest; (PACE, s.32 (7))*

> *A person under arrest for a criminal offence occupies or controls a premises, where a constable reasonably believes that there may be evidence, other than items subject to legal privilege, relating to the offence for which the suspect is held: or to some other arrestable offence which is connected with, or similar to, that offence. (PACE, s.18)*

The Searching of Residential Homes, Day Centres and Other
Premises by the Police

This action must be authorised in writing by an officer of at least the
rank of inspector (PACE, s.18 (4)), unless it is carried out before
taking the person to the police station, if the presence of that person
at a place other than a police station is necessary for the effective
investigation of the offence.

There are occasions when police request entry. The Codes of Practice,
Section B, make the powers of the police explicit when there is a search
with the consent of the staff member in charge of the premises. There
are issues here which are of importance when the staff member agrees
to this action. They need to be aware that when they allow the police
on the premises in such circumstances, they are in control of what the
police do, where they can search, and what they may have access to.
This is important in order to protect the rights of users of the premises
or residents. The following instructions are to be found in the Codes
of Practice, section B, and paragraph numbers refer to this section.

*The staff member in charge of the premises at the time is the
one who is entitled to grant entry. His or her consent must if
practicable, be given in writing to such a search. (4.1)*

*Before seeking consent, the police officer in charge of the
search shall state the purpose of the proposed search, and
inform the person concerned that s/he is not obliged to
consent, and that anything seized may be produced in
evidence. If at the time the person is not suspected of an
offence, the officer shall tell him or her so, when stating the
purpose of the search. (4.2)*

Notes of guidance

Section 4 (A) in Section B of the Codes raises some query about
legitimacy of staff members' right to give access to a resident's room
in certain types of residential establishment. This note states that:

*In the case of a lodging house or similar accommodation, the
search should not be made on the basis solely of the
landlord's consent unless the tenant is unavailable and the
matter is urgent.*

This raises the question of whether certain hostel accommodation for
some client groups would fall into this category. It would seem that
there is a case for a member of staff to refuse admission if the resident

was not there, even if that staff member had keys and access to such a room.

Search under warrant

In addition to the safeguards given under section 16 of PACE outlined previously in these guidelines, the Codes of Practice under Section B give further guidance:

> *Premises may be searched only to the extent necessary to achieve the object of the search...A search under warrant may not continue under the authority of that warrant once all the things specified in it have been found, or the officer in charge of the search is satisfied that they are not on the premises. (COP, B, 5.9)*

> *Searches must be conducted with due consideration to the property and privacy of the occupier of the premises searched, and be of no more disturbance than necessary. Reasonable force may be used only where this is necessary because the co-operation of the occupier cannot be obtained or is insufficient for the purpose. (COP, B, 5.10)*

SEIZURE OF MATERIAL ON THE PREMISES

Seizure of material on premises where social work staff are in charge poses particular questions, especially in relation to where officers will be allowed to search, and what they are allowed to have access to.

A constable who is lawfully on any premises may seize anything which s/he has reasonable grounds for believing:

> *1   has been obtained in consequence of the commission of an offence, and it is necessary to seize it to prevent it being concealed, lost, damaged, altered or destroyed, or*

> *2   is evidence in relation to an offence which s/he is investigating or any other offence, and that it has to be seized in order to prevent evidence being concealed, lost, altered or damaged. (PACE, s.19)*

Computer records can also be accessed under this section but only if they do not contain 'excluded material' (see next section for an explanation of excluded material).

It will be important for the person in charge of an establishment to satisfy him/herself exactly what it is the constable is searching for, and to make sure areas of the establishment which have nothing to do with the search are excluded. For example, in a residential establishment, the residents' rooms would not normally be made available to search if the residents are not directly suspected of involvement in an offence; only the room of the suspected resident, and common areas, will be open to the search.

MATERIAL EXCLUDED FROM SEIZURE UNDER A GENERAL SEARCH

Certain documents, including social work records, are excluded from a constable's power of seizure, unless a special warrant under Schedule 1 of the Act is obtained and presented.

A search warrant authorised by a Circuit Judge in accordance with Schedule 1 of the Act must be issued. (PACE, s.9) The police have no right to see this excluded material without such a warrant. 'Excluded material' under the Act means personal records. These are records which a person has acquired in the course of any trade, profession, or for the purposes of any paid or unpaid office, and which s/he holds in confidence (PACE, s.11). Specifically the Act defines personal records as:

> *Documentary and other records concerning an individual (whether living or dead) who can be identified from them, and relating to*
>
> *(a) his physical and mental health;*
>
> *(b) spiritual counselling;*
>
> *(c) counselling or assistance given to, or to be given to him, for the purposes of his personal welfare, by any voluntary organisation or individual, who by reason of office or occupation has responsibility for his personal welfare; or*

(d) by reason of a Court Order, has responsibilities for his
supervision. (PACE, s.12)

This definition would include index cards and files held by residential, day care and fieldwork staff. Access to such information can only be gained by a Schedule 1 procedure.

Even if such access is gained by the police, there may be letters on file between the client and his/her solicitor. Such material is designated under the Act as 'Items subjects to legal privilege'. These are in no circumstances available to the police and should be removed from any file before police are allowed to see them (PACE, s.10).

SEARCH UNDER SCHEDULE 1 OF THE ACT OR THE PREVENTION OF TERRORISM (TEMPORARY PROVISIONS) ACT 1989 FOR CONFIDENTIAL MATERIAL

When a search takes place under this criterion, an Inspector shall take charge of it, and s/he must ensure it is conducted with discretion and in such a manner as to cause the least possible disruption to any business or other activities carried on in the premises (COP, B, 5.13).

The officer in charge of this search has a right to see indexes to files held on the premises, and they may be inspected for any material sought. The person in charge of the premises must produce the material sought when requested. If the officer in charge of the search believes indexes are incomplete, a more extensive search to the premises can be made (5.14). Requests for such indexes and documents should be directed to the person in authority at the time (NOG, B, 5(B)).

8 COMPLAINTS AGAINST POLICE BEHAVIOUR: PART IX OF THE ACT

A new complaints procedure was introduced by the Act, and now any member of the public (and this definition includes social workers) may make a complaint on behalf of a detainee, with the latter's written permission (PACE, s.84 (4)).

A senior officer will investigate the complaint and try to resolve the matter informally. If this is not possible, the matter will be referred for investigation, possibly to another police force, or possibly to the Police Complaints Authority itself.

As a matter of good practice, any complaint should come from the aggrieved where this is possible. The level of support given by a social worker who is involved would be a matter of professional judgement in each situation, but should in any event include proper advice about the client's rights, help in drafting a letter if necessary, and referral to a Citizen's Advice Bureau or solicitor. The complainant should be advised to seek legal advice immediately, as the timing of a complaint is important. Recourse to a civil action could also be taken.

Where the detainee is not otherwise a client of a social worker, less support will usually be possible. It would probably not be advisable for a social worker to get involved in this manner and referral to a Citizen's Advice Bureau or a solicitor is much more appropriate, with the social worker who acted as an appropriate adult giving independent statements as to the detainee's treatment.

In the first instance a complaint should be addressed to the Chief Constable of the police force concerned (PACE, s.84).

Where complaints are found to have not been justified, the police can sue the complainant.

If a complaint is upheld under the provisions of the Codes of Practice, this does not necessarily mean that the case would be dropped, or that the police's case in court would be diminished. This would be up to the magistrates or judge hearing the facts from the defence solicitor.

INDEX